Internet Power Searching:
The Advanced Manual
2nd Edition

Phil Bradley

BIBLIOTHÈQUES
uOttawa
LIBRARIES

NEAL-SCHUMAN NETGUIDE SERIES

Neal-Schuman Publishers, Inc.
New York   London

Published by
Neal-Schuman Publishers, Inc.
100 Varick Street
New York, NY 10013

Library of Congress Cataloging-in-Publication Data is available.

ISBN 1-55570-447-6

Published simultaneously with Library Association Publishing, London.

Contents

Contents

Contents

Contents

List of figures

Every effort has been made to contact the holders of copyright material reproduced in this text, and thanks are due to them for permission to reproduce the material indicated. If there are any queries please contact the Publishers. (Screenshots which also include the Netscape browser are also Copyright © 2001 Netscape.)

Preface

Welcome to the second edition of *Internet Power Searching: The Advanced Manual*. Since I first became aware of the Internet several years ago I have been fascinated to watch the ways in which it has developed and grown. Since my first faltering footsteps onto it, I have been aware that it is an interesting but frustrating environment to work in. Despite all the hype about how easy it is to use, and how you can find almost anything you want to, I have found that unless you are a skilled searcher this is far from the case. Since the first edition was published, more search engines have been developed, more utilities have been created, and as a result it has become even more difficult and complicated to find what you need quickly. I'm therefore pleased to be able to update the book and hopefully provide more help and advice on making your explorations easier and more successful.

The aim of this book is to help you to search the Internet more effectively by giving you a better understanding of how search engines and related software and utilities work, allowing you to use them to improve your search techniques. I have also given lists of sites you can visit that will help further your understanding, and details of utilities that you can use to make life a little bit easier.

This handbook will be of use to anyone who uses the Internet to find information. It doesn't matter if you are taking your first steps into this new and exciting world or if you are an expert who uses it every day: you will find information, hints, tips, resources and utilities that will be of help. Although I have paid particular attention to the use that information professionals can make of the Internet, you should not feel excluded if you are from another profession –

this book is designed to be of use to everyone who needs to find information quickly!

I have spent a lot of time exploring new and easier ways to obtain information more quickly and effectively by using search engines correctly, and by utilizing some of the many tools available. Here I have tried to explain some of these search engines and tools in detail, with the hope that you too will be able to search for the information you require in as painless a manner as possible.

I also have looked at intelligent agents, mailing lists, newsgroups and so on, and have discussed how they work and why an information person would want to make use of them. In this second edition I have also added some new chapters to assist you in finding images and people. Finally, I have looked into my crystal ball to view some of the ways in which the Internet will be changing the life of the information professional into the next century.

Along the way I've discovered some interesting, sometimes amusing facts about the Internet which I've also shared with you – you will find them in the side panels. It has been an enjoyable trip along the "information superhighway," and although I have not yet reached a final destination (indeed, I doubt that I ever will), I have witnessed many enjoyable sites (and sights!) and met many interesting people.

I ensured that the URLs listed in these pages were current before going to press, but the nature of the Internet is such that some may well have changed when you go to look at them at some point in the future. I hope, however, that your searching abilities will have increased enough to enable you to locate them for yourself!

You can read this manual from cover to cover, or you may prefer to "dip in" and read chapters or sections that appeal to you, or that may help you answer a particular problem or question. At the end of each chapter I have given a list of URLs that I have referred to, and these have also been collated together at the end of the book as Appendix 3. These should prove to be a useful resource in their own right, and I have already referred to them quite a lot in my day-to-day work.

The Internet is changing all our lives, for better or worse, but mostly for the better, I feel. If you embrace the Internet, and learn to use it to its best advantage, I firmly believe that you will be all the richer for it. I hope that this book will prove to be of some help on your own personal journeys.

Acknowledgments

I should like to thank all the organizations and Webmasters who gave me permission to use screenshots of their pages and utilities. All other screenshots are copyright of the original owners.

I would also like to thank all those people within the information industry who have pointed me on the right track, my clients who were understanding in any delays caused to their projects due to the time I spent writing, and to the people I have trained in the past for pointing out new places to visit and new software to explore.

I should also like to pay particular thanks to two people: Helen Carley at Library Association Publishing for encouraging me to write this book and for her help and guidance during the process; and my wife Jill Bradley for her continued help and encouragement.

Internet Power Searching: The Advanced Manual is dedicated, with all my love, to her.

1

An introduction to the Internet

Introduction

The Internet is not a new phenomenon, despite what you may read in the popular or the professional press. It already has a long and involved history; its creation and development profoundly affect the way in which it is used today and indeed how it will be used in the future. As each day passes, it is becoming clear that the Internet already affects or will affect almost every possible area of our lives. Pre-eminent among these changes are the ways in which information professionals view and use information. This chapter outlines some of the important developments of the Internet in order to provide background information. I do not intend to provide a history of the Internet, but if you are interested in this subject you are advised to visit **http://www.yahoo.com/ Computers_and_Internet/Internet/History/**, which provides a list of sites that cover this comprehensively.

An overview of the Internet

I can still remember the first time that I had an opportunity to "surf the net." As an aside, that is the first and last time you'll read that phrase, since it implies skimming over the top, desperately trying to keep your balance and ensure that you don't drown. The skilled user of the Internet knows what information is required and how to find it, retrieve it and go on to make good use of it. Perhaps a better description would be that of an underwater explorer (to adapt the surfing analogy) who is able to plot a course in the ocean to a

HINTS AND TIPS
I have included the addresses or URLs of as many sites as possible to allow you to undertake your own explorations, using the book as your starting-point. In some cases when referring to large subject areas I can only provide a brief overview and hope that you can use the site I refer to for more detail.

specific point, plan and execute a dive, explore the wreck to obtain any treasure, and come back to the surface quickly and safely. This book will show you how to do just that.

When I first looked at the Internet I knew very little other than what I'd been reading in the popular press. My friend Chris had just got an account with an Internet service provider, and invited my wife and myself round for supper and surf. We planned to eat and then spend a couple of hours seeing what was out there. However, supper was not quite ready, so Chris and I began our first ever tour, while my wife read her book. We spent a long while trying to find something that was interesting (this was in the days before the arrival of helpful search engines); we downloaded a video of a NASA space launch, and generally had an enjoyable but frustrating time. We had become so engrossed that we failed to notice that we'd spent four hours in front of the computer, or that supper had burned to a crisp in the oven; my wife meanwhile was fast asleep on the sofa!

Frustrating though it had been, I became hooked on the Internet that evening, and looking back I can recognize that the problems we encountered were inherent in the system and exacerbated by our very limited knowledge. We didn't really know where we were going or how to find what we were looking for, and seemed to spend most of our time visiting one site which led us to a second, then to a third which sent us back to the first one again. It took a long time to download the information we wanted to see; the ten minutes it took us to retrieve that video was rewarded by about ten seconds of moving images! Of course, the Internet has come a long way since then, but users still find it a daunting and confusing place in which to work. For the new user it appears to be entirely chaotic, with neither rhyme nor reason behind it, but perseverance does pay dividends in a reasonably short space of time.

What the Internet is and what it isn't

➤ It's not a single network
Internet is a connection of networks throughout the world. Academic, military, governmental and commercial networks all combine to create the Internet. All the computers

connected to the Internet make use of a common protocol, or way of passing data backwards and forwards, called TCP/IP. Data travels across ordinary telecommunications lines. As a result it is very easy for individuals and organizations to connect to the Internet, thus increasing the amount of information available and also making it more difficult to find it! It also means that it is a robust system; when trying to obtain information from another machine somewhere else in the world, your software will work out the best routes to get from point A to point B, so even if some routes are unavailable you will still normally be able to retrieve the data that is required.

➤ It's both local and global

The Internet isn't interested in geographical locations, and you can find the information that you need regardless of where you happen to be in the world. This is an important change for information professionals. When asked for information in a traditional library setting, an effective searcher will think geographically – is the information in a book on the shelf behind me? If not, is it available elsewhere in the library, or in a sister library down the road, or will it have to be retrieved via an interlibrary loan? All too often this geographical approach is at the expense of authority; while it might ideally make sense to talk to the San Francisco tourist board, for example, it is generally impractical because of the cost, the distance and the time difference. When using the Internet, contacting the appropriate source regardless of geographical location immediately becomes possible; it is simply necessary to find that source and your computer will immediately begin to retrieve data. If you as the information professional feel that the best way of answering a question is to refer the user to a local newspaper, for example, in many cases this is now possible. The Internet enables you to get the most appropriate information quickly, instead of relying on less precise information that may be easily at hand within the traditional library environment. Consequently, global information is available on a local desktop.

➤ It isn't a single entity

The Internet isn't a single uniform resource. It is a collection of different resources, such as the World Wide Web, news-

HINTS AND TIPS
I have tried to keep jargon terms to the minimum, but if you are puzzled by any of them and want more information you may like to visit a glossary of Internet terms at **http://www. matisse.net /files/glossary.html**

groups, mailing lists, real-time "chat" facilities, and much more. An effective searcher will be able to blend all of these different resources into a single collection, using whichever elements are best to answer a query. A business librarian may prefer to use the Web to search financial databases and obtain company reports, while a public librarian may make considerable use of the ready-reference tools that are available, or post a difficult query to a newsgroup, hoping someone else may be able to come up with the answer.

➤ It is possible to use a wide variety of hardware and software

There is no single standard software package used to access the Internet or any of its component parts. In a later chapter we'll look at some of the software which is available, some of which will be appropriate to some users and not others. Effective searchers will create their own library of software tools, specifically designed to provide assistance when seeking information. Similarly, there is no single type of computer which must be used with the Internet. It does of course help if you have a Pentium machine with a large hard disk, lots of memory, a sound card and printer attached, but it is not always necessary. Machines with a lower specification can also give good service without necessarily compromising data retrieval.

➤ It is difficult to say who is in charge

The early networks which eventually combined to create the Internet were very often designed to be open systems that people or organizations could quickly and easily become a part of. Although some control was exerted (to limit participation to academic institutions, for example) no hard and fast rules were laid down. It is true that there are some organizations which are responsible for domain name registration, or for defining the way in which Web pages are written, but as far as the information professional is concerned there is no single authority which decides what information should be made available, or in what form. As a result, individuals and organizations are, by and large, free to do exactly what they wish. Consequently, information may be sparse in some subject areas, while there may be very comprehensive coverage in others; information may be current to within a few moments or it may be years out of date; information may be authoritative or wildly inaccurate; much information will be of no use or may be offensive or illegal in some countries. You have to be able to assess value, currency and authority quickly and accurately without necessarily knowing the publisher, the author, or the extent to which the information has been checked by peer review.

➤ It's fast and effective

The Internet can be a very fast and effective way to communicate with other people or to retrieve information. A company report can be obtained in seconds, a bibliography can be compiled in minutes, and research which would otherwise take days may be completed in hours. As a result, it becomes possible to move from a "just in case" paradigm, in which it is necessary to have a store of information readily on hand in case it is required, to a "just in time" model, where information is not held locally but is retrieved as and when required to meet the needs of a specific inquiry. Effective information professionals can match their information needs to the availability of data on the Internet, and as a result may decide that there is no need to subscribe to a range of printed newspapers, for example, since many of them are readily available on the Web, together with archival information.

➤ It is easy to talk to individuals or groups

Usenet newsgroups and mailing lists allow people with similar interests to keep in touch, to share knowledge, to express opinions or even just to gossip! Communities of interest are created which facilitate the free flow of information, freed from the confines of time or geographical location. This allows you to make contact with others around the world, to disseminate information to large numbers of people in ways previously not possible, and to draw on the experience of peers and experts in fields that you may never have known about before.

➤ It's not all hard work

Information on the Internet covers almost literally every single subject that you could think of, plus a few more besides.

DID YOU KNOW?
Although no one organization "controls" the Internet, the W3 Consortium is an interna-tional industry consortium which aims to develop common protocols to aid the growth and expansion of the Internet. They can be found at **http://www.w3c.org**

Professional information (however you care to define that) and personal or hobby information sit happily side by side, and it is as easy to discover the results of last night's lottery as it is to locate companies that sell chemical compounds. Even a small information center is in a position to provide access to resources which previously would have fallen outside its remit. This does, however, bring with it the associated problem of ensuring that terminals are used to retrieve appropriate information, and not to download glamour pictures or worse!

➤ It's not just for "geeks"

Up until four or five years ago access to information on the Internet was by using a variety of tools that were less than user-friendly. Veronica, Archie and Gopher services located and retrieved information, but these tools were difficult for end-users to master. Now, however, graphical interfaces, search engines and intelligent agents ensure that even novice users can quickly locate and retrieve information. This ease of use does come at a price: end-users will increasingly require training in the critical assessment of the results they are achieving and the authority of the information they have obtained.

➤ It's not well organized

Since no one "owns" the Internet, everyone can do almost exactly as they please. No centralized authority means that people will publish the same information in different formats, incorrect or out-of-date information appears as well as accurate current information, and organizations and individuals will arrange their data and access to it in ways that please them. Flexibility on the part of the searcher is therefore paramount, coupled with the ability quickly to identify how information is arranged and to locate relevant data within a site.

➤ It's growing at an enormous rate

There is little point in attempting to provide figures for the number of people who are connected to the Internet, simply because it is almost impossible to do, and even if it could be done, the figure would be very out of date by the time you read this. A generally agreed rule of thumb is that the Internet is doubling in size every year, in terms of users and Web pages. This means that information professionals have to work very hard to keep up to date with what is happening in this area. In order to be effective it is necessary to spend several hours a week locating new sites and trying new software. However, there are resources which can help in this process, and I have provided a list of some of them in Chapter 15.

If some of the terms used above make little sense at the moment, don't worry, because I'll be going into more detail on all these issues later on in the book. For now I'd like to provide you with further background on the different areas of the Internet I discuss in later chapters.

Search engines

One of the characteristics of the Internet is the speed at which it has grown in the last four or five years. No one is quite sure of the size of the Internet or of the World Wide Web, and I've seen lots of conflicting statistics, most of which are quite out of date. However, a figure that I've heard often quoted is five billion Web pages, and I am happy to go along with that. Even if it is incorrect at the time of writing, by the time this book has been published and is in your hands I would expect it to be accurate or even an underestimate.

In the early days of the Internet it was reasonably easy to find information or datafiles using a variety of software that was usually command driven: that is, you needed to type in the command you wanted executed, rather than using a graphical interface. However, with the proliferation of data brought about by the growth of the Web, these systems with such names as Archie, Gopher and Veronica became increasingly unable to cope. In order to overcome the lack of retrieval facilities, a number of organizations and individuals began to create their own software for searching and retrieving information. Unfortunately, very few of them had any kind of library or information background, so although they were (and are) doing a very sophisticated job of finding and indexing all that information, the early implementations were quite crude. They were not designed for trained searchers, but for people who had never done a literature search in their lives, and as a

DID YOU KNOW?
If you want to find out how many people currently have access to the internet you may wish to look at the Irresponsible Internet Statistics Generator at **http://www.anamorph. com/docs/stats/stats.html**

result they did not make any use of Boolean operators, proximity searching, wildcards, truncation or any of the other things that we take for granted. Users simply entered any keywords that they felt were appropriate, and the search engines would retrieve hits based on their perceived relevance.

Over the course of time some of these search engines have hardly moved forward at all, and still the only way of finding appropriate Web pages is to throw as many search terms at them as possible and hope that you are lucky! However, some of the others have been through many new versions and are achieving the kind of sophistication that we take for granted when searching an online or CD-ROM-based database.

As information professionals the world over know, there is more than one way to catalog or classify a book, and there is certainly more than one way to index the Internet! Chapter 2 explains in some detail how the different types of search engines work, and the advantages and disadvantages of using them. The next three chapters then look at particular search engines, how they can be used effectively and when they should be used.

Commercial databases

The history of commercial databases deserves a study in its own right, since the production of them, their use and subsequent developments closely match technological advances. However, this is not the place for such a discussion, so I will restrict my comments here to the way that the Internet has affected online commercial databases. As we will see later, database publishers are starting to make their databases available via the Internet. This is the case for traditional online publishers, and also increasingly for CD-ROM publishers. This means that the information professional has yet another avenue to explore when providing data access to the end-user.

This is a logical extension from the early provision of CD-ROM databases in the information center, since it is a way of moving data out of the libraries and onto people's desktops. Moreover, it is further influencing the job of the information professional, who is moving away from being the "gatekeeper," or the person who goes away and obtains information for users, towards being the "facilitator," who no longer performs the search, but establishes systems and trains users to obtain the required data for themselves.

The provision of commercial databases on the Internet is closely associated with electronic commerce. Once publishers can make their data available in this way, more flexible and varied pricing systems can be introduced. Users may, for example, buy a block of units that can be spent on retrieving any records from a publisher's collection of databases, or it may be preferable to continue to subscribe to a particular product. Publishers are going to have to work harder to keep market share, by providing value-added services, and we will explore some of the challenges facing the publishers, the information professionals and the end-users in more detail in Chapter 9.

Virtual libraries and gateways

As we shall see, one of the problems of using search engines is that they return all the data they can retrieve indiscriminately; the search engines are unable to make any qualitative judgments on the value or authority of the information they find. One of the advantages of the Internet is that it is very easy to publish information, and unfortunately that is one of its greatest disadvantages as well; no one owns the Internet, so no one is able to say "this is good" or "this is bad," and in any case, what is good to one person is bad to another. The whole question of authority is one which is mentioned to me at every training session I give, and so in Chapter 10 I have explained some ways in which the level of authority of a particular document can be quickly assessed.

Information professionals have been taking an important role in this area, and over the last few years a large number of virtual libraries have been established. These attempt to gather together links to Websites with authoritative, current, trustworthy and useful information. As a result, they are a very useful set of resources, which are all too often sadly ignored or badly publicized. The people who maintain virtual libraries have done a considerable amount of work for others in their subject areas, and these resources can provide a useful starting point for searches. Indeed, it may not be necessary to look anywhere else for the information which is required.

Virtual libraries are yet another example of the librarian

acting as facilitator, and they can save searchers a lot of time by directing them to hard information. In Chapter 10 I explore the concepts behind them, and list some of those which are particularly useful, as well as explaining how they can best be utilized.

Intelligent agents

Search engines of all types, commercial databases, virtual libraries and gateways all have one thing in common: you have to visit them to find the information that is required. This is commonly referred to as "pull technology"; the information has to be pulled down from a server somewhere. This may be perfectly acceptable for a lot of searches, but in situations where it is necessary to provide a current awareness service it very quickly becomes time consuming and laborious.

Intelligent agents help to overcome this problem by actively seeking out information that is needed, and they can be used to keep you up to date with what is happening in a particular subject area. Some of the most recent innovative agents can also be taught about the information that is particularly useful in any given situation, and are intelligent enough to go and explore the Internet on your behalf, sift what they find and present you with a small, focused and accurate collection of data.

There are many different types of intelligent agent, ranging from those which merely collate information in broad subject areas and make it available to you via a Web page (very often linked to specific search engines) to those that can be trained and which will then act independently on your behalf. Chapter 11 covers these agents in some detail, and explores the way in which they can be used to make searching an easier and more enjoyable experience.

Newsgroups and mailing lists

If the Internet is about anything, it is about people being able to talk to people. Much work is currently being undertaken in the fields of video conferencing and Internet telephony, for example, and though they have a long way to go before being fully functional, they are a good indication of the importance we all put on being able to talk to each other when and where we want.

Newsgroups and mailing lists are not as visually exciting or as "sexy" as these recent innovations, but they have a long history, and are still perhaps the best way we have at present to talk to each other across the Internet. Unfortunately, they are also an under-used resource, perhaps because they have been around since the early days of the Internet. In Chapter 12 I go into much more detail about what exactly newsgroups and mailing lists are, and explain how they can be of real assistance to the information professional. I give you some pointers on the different ways they can be used (both in technical and professional terms), and what software is required.

The information mix

As I have already said, the Internet is not one thing: it is a collection of different types of software and resources, used by many millions of people, all of whom have their own particular reasons to be using it. Never was this more true than when looking at how the information profession utilizes this collection of resources.

As a profession we are faced with an almost bewildering array of resources: traditional book-based sources, online databases, CD-ROM and DVD technology, search engines, virtual libraries, newsgroups, mailing lists, intelligent agents – the list could go on and on. However, our key role has not changed; information has to be gathered, sifted, checked, and made available in one form or another for our users. The question of how this is done, though, is becoming more and more complex as each new facility is made available.

Once you have explored some of the sites I mention, and have installed and become familiar with the software needed, the next step is to try and make some sense of it all. As users also engage in the same process, and technology continues its rapid development, this problem becomes more acute. It is necessary to try to blend and mix these resources together into a coherent package which is appropriate for your own user community. Where should the information be found? Should information be made available in a variety of formats? Is it possible to dispense with some traditional information resources and replace them with something else? How can users be encouraged to find information for themselves? What advances do we need to be at least aware of, if not actively planning to embrace them? I attempt to answer these questions in Chapter 13, and also point out where the Internet is perhaps leading us.

Better searching

A full understanding of the Internet and its resources is obviously invaluable, and a searcher cannot work effectively without this knowledge. I hope that this book will help you obtain this understanding, but a broad overview is only part of the picture. Sometimes it is necessary to explore some of the minutiae of systems and software. It is surprising just how much time can be saved daily by reducing each search by two minutes, or by using a shortcut here or there. In Chapter 14 I've collected together a number of hints and tips that should make searching and using the Internet a little bit easier and a little bit faster. I would estimate that you may be able to save several hours each week by incorporating them into your working methods.

Better software

The Internet, and particularly the World Wide Web, is constantly growing and increasing in complexity as people explore new possibilities. In its early stages, the Web was text-based, but it did not take long before still images, animated graphics, sound and multimedia were brought into play. Browsers are becoming equally sophisticated, with ever greater functionality.

Consequently, Web designers are always pushing the boundaries of what is possible, and commercial organizations, always seeking revenue, are providing ever more software to take advantage of the Web. In order to remain effective and to gain the most out of the system it is necessary to keep as up to date as possible, and the only way to do this is to install new software and to upgrade older versions.

In Chapter 15 I look at resources on the Internet that can help you in this area, and examine in more detail some packages which can make a very real difference to searching and using the Internet.

Where to go next?

The speed at which the Internet is growing means that it is not possible to stop still; if you try and do that you will find that you are out of date within a matter of days. The Internet is a little like a treadmill; once you have got on it and started to walk, it becomes difficult to get off it. Worse than that, the treadmill just goes faster and faster, and you have to run harder just to keep from falling behind. There are a number of Internet resources that are worth using to help keep you current, as well as organizations providing training courses. Chapter 15 also goes into detail on these resources, with the intention of ensuring that you don't fall behind – or if you do, that you are able to catch up again!

Summary

In this introductory chapter I have identified some of the key elements that affect the way in which the information professional is able to use the Internet, and have alerted you to the major areas that this book covers. I expect that you will find some chapters to be of more immediate interest than others, so feel free to explore those; each chapter stands on its own, and while they do make reference to each other, you can read them in any order that you wish.

URLs mentioned in this chapter

http://www.yahoo.com/Computers_and_Internet/
　　Internet/History/
http://www.matisse.net/files/glossary.html
http://www.w3c.org
http://www.anamorph.com/docs/stats/stats.html

Part 1

Mining the Internet for information

2

An introduction to search engines

Introduction

The Internet is often referred to (in my opinion incorrectly) as the "Information Superhighway."

The term gives the impression that it is fast and effective, getting you quickly from A to B in the twinkling of an eye. Furthermore, it implies that the ride is going to be a smooth one, with no bumps or potholes, and certainly no chance that you are going to break down.

Unfortunately, nothing could be further from the truth. In point of fact, I think a closer and rather more accurate analogy is that of the library I would expect to find in the type of gothic house you see in horror films: huge and rambling, with long corridors leading off into the middle of nowhere, small rooms packed with frequently used material in little order and yet other places shrouded in darkness from which one can hear rather nasty noises. The whole grand edifice is presided over by a half-insane librarian who is constantly coming up with new classification and cataloging schemes. He implements them on a few hundred titles before thinking of a new idea, and begins again with a different scheme on some new materials which have just been dumped in no order on the floor. Meanwhile, the minions of our insane librarian are busily working in different rooms, constantly arranging and rearranging their own collections, without reference to each other, and each convinced that they have the best collection and best scheme for its arrangement.

Unfair? Yes, perhaps it is, but only a little. We've already seen just how fast the World Wide Web is growing, and it is

DID YOU KNOW?
You can find the origins of this phrase, and many other quotes, by pointing your browser to
http://www.quoteland.co m/index.html

easy to let your eyes glaze over at the sheer amount of data that we're talking about. The Web *is* large and it *is* growing at a tremendous speed, and gathering speed under its own anarchic mass, but strangely enough it is, in the main, going in one direction. As a result, it is possible to impose some control over it and to put some structures in place. Chief among these are the different search engines, which prove to be of great assistance in allowing us to quickly find the exact piece of data that we require, sometimes in less time than it takes to articulate and type in the query.

I am not going to pretend that the search engines are perfect – very far from it! As we will discover, they all have their own shortcomings, and we are a long way from having a perfect interface or comprehensive index to the Internet. However, until we finally reach that holy grail we have to work with the tools that are available to us, and in this chapter I am going to give you an overview of the way in which the search engines actually do their jobs; the more you understand about search engines the easier they are to use and the more effective they become.

The rise of the search engine

I'll start by asking you a question: "How many search engines do you think there are out there?" The chances are that your immediate reaction would be to give me a figure in the region of perhaps a dozen or so. If you've just read the previous chapter, you'll already have learned not to underestimate the size of the Internet and the speed at which it grows, so you may be a little more confident in giving a larger figure, perhaps in the region of 400 or 500. You would still be a long way short of the mark, as there are somewhere in the region of 20,000 search engines that you can choose to assist you in finding the information that you require.

If you find this figure just too remarkable to believe, I'd ask you to hold back on your skepticism for a moment or two. While my question was not exactly a trick, I expect that you were thinking of one specific type of search engine, the type that attempts to index the whole of the Internet, such as *AltaVista* or *Yahoo!*. If you'd said a dozen or so of that type you'd be a little nearer to a correct answer, though you'd still be out by rather a large number. When I posed the question I was thinking much more broadly than just that generic type of search engine – I was including lots of smaller engines which may only search one particular site, or one particular resource, such as a dictionary. Once you redefine search engines more broadly, the figure of 20,000 becomes less implausible. If you are still looking at this page in disbelief, I'll point you towards a couple of search engines which list search engines as one of their functions – *All-in-One Search Page* at **http://www.allonesearch.com** and *Ixquick*™ at **http://www.ixquick.com**, which I'll look at in more detail in Chapter 5.

Let's discuss this business of definition in a little more detail. There are basically five different types of search engine available to you:

➤ free-text search engines
➤ index- or directory-based search engines
➤ multi- or meta-search engines (both terms are used inter changeably)
➤ natural-language search engines
➤ resource- or site-specific search engines.

Free-text search engines

Free-text search engines are very easy to describe. You can simply search for any single word, a number of words or in some cases a phrase. You are not limited in any way as to your choice – you may wish to search for the name of a company, a line of poetry, a number, a person's name, a foreign language term, just about anything.

This approach has both advantages and disadvantages, as you would expect. Free-text search engines are very useful if you know exactly what you are looking for, or if you are looking for a concept which can be defined in a small number of words. They are less useful if you want a broad overview of a subject, or are searching in an area that you don't know very well and consequently have no idea as to the best terms to use. There are a great many free-text search engines available for you to use, and we'll look at some of them in later chapters, but for now if you want to break off

DID YOU KNOW?
It is a common practice for organizations trying to sell pornography on the Internet to register site names which are similar to those of existing, reputable search engines, perhaps only differing by a single letter. Consequently you should take care when typing Web addresses, and particularly those of search engines, in case you arrive at a site which contains information you'd really rather not see!

HINTS AND TIPS

If you search for two words, such as President Bush, most free-text search engines will translate that as a search for President OR Bush, but will give a higher relevance ranking to those sites which contain both words.

reading and try one out I'd suggest that you go and have a look at *AltaVista* at **http://www.altavista.com**.

Most of the free-text search engines are unfortunately quite primitive in their approach, and if you have used online or CD-ROM-based resources you might be a little surprised. With a few notable exceptions, all that you can do is to type in a series of words. You cannot use Boolean operators, truncation or wildcard symbols, and you may not even be able to search for a phrase. Free-text search engines are often aimed at the lowest common denominator, which is people who have never done any kind of searching before.

Relevance ranking

You may therefore wonder how you are able to retrieve any information of value from your searches, and the answer is that these engines use relevance ranking when they display results on the screen. They employ a series of complicated algorithms to order the hits into a list with the sites that they think you will be most interested in at the top, with the less appropriate sites lower down the list. Search engine designers all have their own ideas as to the most appropriate methods of ranking sites (which they change on a tiresomely regular basis), which means that you will get an entirely different set of records from different engines, even if you are using exactly the same search criteria.

I've listed some of the criteria that are used by free-text search engines below, but please note that not all search engines will use all of these criteria, and even if they do they may well give different weighting to them.

HINTS AND TIPS

The meta-tag element is a hidden element on a page which is seen by the search engine but not the viewer. It is a way in which the author of the page can define key terms and concepts contained within it. Search engines often use the meta-data to calculate the page's ranking in the returned results.

➤ word/term/phrase appears within the meta-tag element
➤ word/term/phrase appears in the title of the Web page
➤ word/term/phrase can be found in a main heading or sub-heading of a page
➤ the number of times the word/term/phrase appears in the body of the text
➤ the number of links from other Web pages.

Index- or directory-based search engines

These search engines take a rather different approach to providing you with information on the sites that you might want to visit. Their emphasis is on classifying information under a series of major subject headings, and then subdividing these into a tree structure of more specific headings, and sites are listed as appropriate in this directory structure. If this approach sounds familiar, that is because it is, as anyone who has ever used a library classification scheme will know.

The advantages of this approach are obvious. The subject headings and subheadings can be used to guide the users through the vast mass of information until they are able to locate exactly the right section which covers the area that they are interested in. An in-depth knowledge of the subject is not required, since the users can stop drilling down through the tree at any point, check one or two sites to see that they are in the right area, and then continue to focus and re-focus until they get to a reasonably small number of sites which can then be viewed individually if needed. Probably the most famous of these index search engines is Yahoo!, and you may wish to break off from reading to go and have a look at it – Yahoo! is to be found at **http://www.yahoo.com.**

You will not be surprised to know, however, that there are also disadvantages inherent in this approach, and these lie in the initial construction of the headings structure, which may well show up individual biases. For example, if you are looking at *Yahoo!*, one of the main subject headings together with its subheadings is:

Government
    Elections
    Military
    Law
    Taxes

American readers are probably looking at this and scratching their heads, wondering what is wrong with it. This is perfectly understandable, because from an American point of view there is nothing wrong with it. However, a British reader might look slightly askance at the subheadings, since we would expect to find some of them elsewhere in the hierarchy. *Yahoo!* has attempted to overcome this particular problem by providing country-specific versions of the index, as we shall discover later. The basic point still stands, however: when you use an index search engine you are at the mercy of the people who put the structure into place. If you assume that a subject is going to be found under one series of subheadings, you may spend a lot of time drilling down into one section of the index, when what you want is to be found elsewhere. To use the example above, a logical assumption might be to look for information on the last British general election somewhere in that Government/Elections hierarchy, but in actual fact information on this subject is found under Regional/Countries/United Kingdom.

Many of the organizations which have produced index-based search engines have recognized that this may be a problem for their users, and have created a free-text search box which can be used to quickly identify exactly where within a hierarchy the users will find information about their subject of interest. We'll see how some of the major engines have done this in Chapter 4.

Multi- or meta-search engines

The next type of search engine isn't really a search engine at all, since a multi-search engine doesn't actually search anything itself. Instead it takes your query and passes it on to a selected group of search engines. Once the results start coming in from these individual search engines, a multi-search engine displays the results on the screen. The more advanced engines will collate the results, removing duplicates, and put them into some sort of sensible order.

Multi-search engines are useful if you want to try and obtain a comprehensive listing of Websites that cover a particular subject. Individual search engines may well not be fully comprehensive, and one may index sites that another has missed and vice versa. Searching each of them individually is going to take time: you must locate the URL, visit the engine, input your search, wait for the results and then visit the pages you find useful before repeating the whole process somewhere else. Using a multi-search engine means that you only have to visit one page, and all the results are brought back to your screen, therefore limiting the amount of work that you have to do.

Unfortunately, this strength is also a major weakness of a multi-search engine. Since you are submitting your search to a number of different search engines, they all have to be able to understand the syntax that you are using. Therefore either you have to know that each of the engines understands the symbols used to run a phrase search, for example (which means more work for you), or you are limited to just putting in various keywords without being able to focus your search more tightly. Some of the more sophisticated multi-search engines are now able to translate your query into the correct syntax for each search engine, but this cannot be guaranteed, so you should check, rather than automatically rely on this happening.

There is a second type of multi-search engine, which is perhaps even less like a search engine than the type that I have described above. These engines simply provide you with links through to lots of other search engines, without even giving you the opportunity to input search terms to be for-warded to them. If I were being pedantic I would refer to sites such as this as "launchpad" sites, rather than search sites in their own right. They can be very useful, however, by providing you with links to search engines and other resources which you might otherwise have never found at all – or, if my experience is anything to go by, which you would have found the day after you really needed them!

If you are keen to try out a multi-search engine, you could visit the *All-in-One Search Page* at **http://www.allonesearch. com**, or if you want to have a look at the second type of engine, pay a visit to *search.com* at **http://www.search.com**.

Natural-language search engines

This is a very small category with only very few engines; the most popular is probably *Ask Jeeves* at **http//www.aj.com** or the British version at **http://www.ask.co.uk**. Search engines in this category will take your search terms and will attempt to map them to other terms as well, so a search for "tax revenues" will also look for financial, business and economic information, for example.

They can be very useful if you are having real problems finding information; for example, I was able to find a list of gases that are partially soluble in water by asking the question "which gases are partially soluble in water?" I doubt that I would have been able to find that information as quickly or as easily using any other search engine.

Resource- or site-specific search engines

The final category of search engines is perhaps the largest, but paradoxically the least used, probably as a result of their diversity. A resource-specific engine may well have been created simply to search one particular resource, such as the Bible, a dictionary or an encyclopedia. There is very little which can be said generally about these engines, since they are all very different to look at and to use. One point which it is important to make, however, is that generally the resources which they index are not indexed by other, more general search engines, and the reasons for this will become clear in the next section of this chapter. Since these resources are site-specific it is not possible to point to a complete listing of them, but the *All-in-One Search Page* does provide you with access to a number of them.

One type of resource-specific search engine which is worth mentioning here in a little detail is what is generally referred to as a "people finder" or "people searcher." These engines will, as the name implies, find people on the Internet for you, a little like directory inquiries. You obviously need to know a little bit about the person you're looking for, such as their name, or part of their name (this isn't as silly as it sounds, since you can find references on the Internet to me as Phil Bradley, Philip Bradley or philb), where they come from (either their geographical location or where they post messages from), and any other information you have available. A people searcher will then attempt to locate individuals in its database that match the information you have provided, and will list them for you, thus allowing you to contact them. Usually the e-mail address is given, but in some cases you can also discover their geographical address and even phone number. I'll take a more in-depth look at these in Chapter 8.

How search engines work

In order to use these resources effectively, it is necessary to have some background knowledge of how they work. Most of them make use of "spider" or "robot" utilities which spend their time crawling the Web looking for new sites, or sites which have changed since the spider last visited. When they find new or updated pages, they copy this information back home to be included in an updated version of the index at the search engine site. The spider will also follow any new links which it finds and repeat the process until it cannot find any more new pages, at which point it will retrace its steps and follow a new route.

This has a number of implications as far as the searcher is concerned. Given the size of the World Wide Web, this is a full-time job, and even the fastest computers have trouble keeping up with the flood of new pages onto the Web. This has been overcome to a certain extent in that Website authors can contact search engines to inform them of new or updated pages which should be included in the indexes. As a general rule, priority is given to checking these pages, and in some cases they can be checked and added to a search engine index within a matter of seconds. However, if the author does not do this, it may take several weeks or even months for the pages to be located and indexed.

Search engine database currency

Consequently, when a search is run using a search engine, the results will only be a snapshot of the Web as it existed at some time in the past. That might be a matter of moments, or it may be days in some cases. Depending on the subject you are looking for, this may be a major problem or a minor inconvenience, but it should always be kept in mind. It may be necessary in some cases to change your overall search strategy completely; if you are looking for information on the latest earthquake, or the death of a celebrity, you will probably get the information you need by checking a newspaper Website which is updated hourly, rather than by relying on some of the more general search engines that I have discussed. To be fair to them, however, within hours they were

DID YOU KNOW?

It is difficult to work out which are the most popular search engines, but two companies (Media Metrix and Nielsen//NetRatings) both conduct studies in this area, and for December 2000 listed the major search engines in the following order of popularity: Yahoo!, MSN, Go (Infoseek), Lycos, Netscape. More details can be obtained from **http://www.searchengine watch.com**

DID YOU KNOW?

Approximately 81 new Web pages are published every second.

indexing and returning Website addresses which related to the death of Diana, Princess of Wales.

Unfortunately, while search engines may be slow to provide searchers with new sites, they will also retain information on Web pages that no longer exist. It is quite common for an author to delete a page from a Website when it is no longer required, and the only way that the search engines can discover this is to try to re-visit the page in order to re-index it. When an engine cannot find the page after a number of attempts, it will assume that the page no longer exists, and it will be deleted from the engine's index of sites. However, since there may well be a gap of weeks or even months between the author deleting the page and the engine discovering this, it will continue to include the page in the lists of results which are returned from a search. Do not be surprised, therefore, if you attempt to visit a page, only to be given an error message that states that the page cannot be found. Make a note of the page and try again later, but if it fails every time the page in question has probably been deleted by the author or moved to another location.

Not all search engines work on the principle of spiders, and a good example of one which does not is *Yahoo!*. This search engine requires Web page authors to visit their site and register their pages into the most appropriate category (or categories) that *Yahoo!* covers. (If this isn't clear, don't worry – either visit *Yahoo!* yourself, or skip to Chapter 4 to get some more information on *Yahoo!*.) Therefore, you are to some extent at the mercy of the authors, because if they index their pages incorrectly or obscurely this will lessen your chance of finding them when doing a search.

Meta-search engines do not index pages themselves in either of the ways described above. As mentioned earlier, they simply connect to search engines and run searches. The results obtained therefore rely on the ability of the engines used to provide current and comprehensive results.

Who owns the search engines?

Search engines are created by anyone who has the time, money and skill to devote to creating one. The Internet has few rules and regulations, so anyone can (to a greater or lesser extent) do exactly what they want to, and some organizations and individuals have decided that, for a variety of reasons, they wish to establish and maintain search engines for people to use. Most engines will provide you with some sort of background as to their origins in case you are interested in such things, but in most cases they were created because someone wanted to; it really is as simple as that. Some organizations could see there were commercial possibilities to be made out of having a Website that gets visited thousands, if not millions of times a day.

How much do they cost to use?

Search engines take a considerable amount of time to establish and maintain. This requires full-time staff, expensive computer equipment, advertising and communications. It may therefore come as something of a surprise to discover that there are very few engines that charge end-users to search them. You are free to connect to your search engine of choice, interrogate the database and move on to view sites that interest you. In the training sessions that I run, people often express amazement that all of this information is given away freely, so if you are also surprised by this, do not worry – you are not alone!

Advertising

The answer to the question is, however, very simple, and can be summed up in a single phrase – "advertising revenue." Despite what I have just said about organizations giving away information and use of their facilities, the Internet is commercially driven, and this is best demonstrated by looking at the number of advertisements on Websites offering a whole host of products. Almost all search engines include banner advertisements from other organizations enticing viewers to visit the sponsoring site; and once you visit, you will be faced with some very skillful attempts to part you from your money. Advertisers work on the theory of maximum exposure for maximum profits, and nowhere is this more evident than on a search-engine page. If an advertiser has a product for sale which costs $100 and places an advertisement for it on a site which is visited 10,000,000 times a day (which is not uncommon), if only 1% of people who see the banner visit the advertiser's site, and only 1% of them buy the product, that means a revenue stream of $100,000 per day! Consequently, they will be prepared to pay a reasonably large sum to the owner of a site that commands that many visitors.

Advertising placement

The subject of Internet commerce is much too large for the scope of this book, so I will not say very much more about it, other than to point out that it is possible for the astute searcher sometimes to make use of the advertisements. Placement of advertisements is becoming more sophisticated now, and if you run a search on some search engines for keywords such as "gardens, gardening, flowers" it is likely that the banner advertisement which gets displayed on the results screen will be for a site that sells gardening equipment, or it may be for an Internet florist, for example. Consequently, if you want to find such organizations, it could be quite useful to spend a few moments browsing the linking site.

To generate the maximum advertising revenue, it is in the best interests of the owners of search engines to encourage as many visitors as possible, which means having increasingly powerful search software, easy and advanced interfaces, and so on. Indeed, many of the larger search engines are now offering free e-mail addresses for life, Web space, personalized news services, and anything else they can think of to encourage visitors to return time and time again. Therefore, although in one sense searching is entirely free, in another sense you do actually pay by having to download an advertisement every time you view a page of results.

Summary

In this chapter I have outlined the major types of search engine and how they can be used. In order to search the Internet successfully it is necessary to match the search you wish to do against the type of engine and your level of knowledge of the subject. Each search engine will provide different results, based on the data contained in their indexes and the way in which they rank results for relevance.

None of the search engines is perfect, and all have their own particular advantages and disadvantages. The successful searcher will have a good understanding of the rationale behind their design and working methods. In later chapters I look at the different types of engine in more detail, and focus on a number of particularly important and popular ones.

URLs mentioned in this chapter

http://www.quoteland.com/index.html
http://www.allonesearch.com
http://www.ixquick.com
http://www.altavista.com
http://www.yahoo.com
http://www.aj.com
http://www.ask.co.uk
http://www.searchenginewatch.com
http://www.amazon.com

3

Free-text search engines

Introduction

In this chapter I look in more detail at free-text search engines; how they can assist the searcher, search methodologies and so on. I focus on one free-text search engine in particular, AltaVista, but also point you towards others which work in a similar fashion, namely Lycos, HotBot, and Northern Light.

Free-text search engines:

➤ will accept any term the user wishes to search for
➤ can search for terms in any combination
➤ can search for phrases as well as single words
➤ allow users considerable flexibility in choosing how to search.

AltaVista

AltaVista is one of the best known and oldest search engines available on the Internet (the other being *Yahoo!*) and was launched on 15 December 1995 at **http://www.altavista. com**. On its first day it received 300,000 visits; it is now "hit" over 20,000,000 times per day. The AltaVista Search Public Service was the brainchild of researchers at Digital Equipment Corporation's Palo Alto Laboratory, and research into the project to index the World Wide Web began in the spring of 1995. Work began in earnest during the summer of that year, and the whole project was up and running within six months.

The aim of the *AltaVista* service is to index the entire

DID YOU KNOW?
AltaVista was the code name of the project and was not adopted as the name of the service until two days before it was launched.

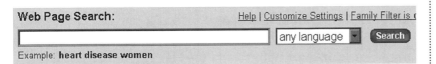

Fig. 3.1   *'AltaVista' search box*
© 2001 AltaVista Company

World Wide Web, and the *AltaVista* team has estimated that they have indexed over 350,000,000 Web pages, making it one of the largest of the search engines. In theory, therefore, the majority of Web pages are stored by *AltaVista* on their servers, making it a good backup system, but I'm not sure that this would be a good thing to rely on!

Searching *AltaVista*: easy search

When *AltaVista* is displayed on your screen the most important element is the search box as shown in Figure 3.1.

To begin with, we'll ignore everything other than the white rectangle, which is the place in which you type your query. Since *AltaVista* is a free-text search engine, you can type in anything you wish, and it will attempt to find Web pages which match your search criteria. Please keep in mind that *AltaVista* will automatically OR searches together unless you tell it otherwise. This inevitably leads to large results, but don't let this put you off. *AltaVista* will rank the Web pages it retrieves for relevance according to its own algorithms, by displaying what it thinks are the best possible matches first, with the less relevant ones further down the page.

Narrowing a search using truncation

As a result, a search using only one or two terms is not going to work very well, since the searcher is not giving the search engine very much to go on. A better search strategy would therefore be to include as many different terms as possible, since one of the ways in which *AltaVista* works is to give the highest relevance score to Web pages which include all of your terms, or failing that, which include the greatest number of them. Consequently, if you were doing a search for '*Jaguar cars*' it would make sense to do a search for '*Jaguar car cars automobile automobiles vehicle vehicles*' and so on.

HINTS AND TIPS

The Boolean operators are AND, OR, NOT, although some search engines require users to write AND NOT rather than NOT. They are the basis on which any search for two or more terms is run. 'Cat AND dog' will give a set of results which contain both terms; 'cat OR dog' will give a larger set in which the results have to contain only one of the two words; 'cat AND NOT dog' will limit the results to records that contain only the word 'cat', but not the word 'dog'

Alternatively, I could have saved myself a few keystrokes by using the asterisk '*', forcing the search engine to look for any words that start with the letters chosen, and any others which appear after the '*'. If I had truncated my search term at *car** *AltaVista* would have found matches for: *car, cars, cart, career*, and so on. However, in this case I would have retrieved far too many records which had nothing at all to do with cars, so while I would have saved a few moments typing I would have wasted more time in the long run having to skip over records that had no relevance to my search.

Weighting search terms

AltaVista does give your first term greater weight than the other terms. However, that would not stop it from finding a site which contained all the terms requested with the exception of *Jaguar* and deciding that such a site was more appropriate than a site which just contained the key word you really wanted to find. We therefore need some way of telling *AltaVista* that some terms are more important than others, and to do this we use the plus (+) symbol. This tells *AltaVista* that it must find sites which contain that particular word, with the other chosen terms being of less importance. Our search strategy would now look like this: '*+Jaguar car cars automobile automobiles vehicle vehicles*'. It will come as no surprise that we can also use the minus (-) symbol to exclude words which we are not interested in. Looking through the results which are returned from the above search I would not be surprised to find sites which use the term jaguar as the large wild animal, so I could include *-cat -animal* in the search strategy as well. Our search, which has now expanded to: '*+Jaguar car cars automobile automobiles vehicle vehicles -cat -animal*', is getting rather long and cumbersome.

Phrase searching

We do have another option available to use, which is to look for a phrase. *AltaVista* makes use of double quote marks (" ") to indicate that we wish to search for a particular phrase. As a result I may find that my search yields better results if I do a search for '"*Jaguar cars*"', which is shorter and neater, leading to a smaller and more appropriate set of results. I can now ignore the possibility of retrieving Web pages which refer to the wild animal, since it is unlikely that pages would refer to both the car and the animal, or if they do it will only be a very small number. You'll also note that I'm using a capital J in my search, and there is a very good reason for this. If you use a lower-case character *AltaVista* will automatically look for and retrieve both lower- and upper-case versions, but if you use upper-case *AltaVista* restricts itself to finding exact matches. This is very useful if you are searching for someone whose name is Brown, for example, in that you can, generally speaking, limit your search to surnames rather than for brown-colored things. (It does not exclude the possibility of finding the word 'Brown' at the start of a sentence referring to colored objects, but we can't have everything!)

Refining searches

Although I have been able to limit my search to a smaller number of results, I will still be retrieving a set which is much bigger than I want to have to work my way through. However, *AltaVista* has also considered that, and once you have run your search you will notice that there is an option to search within these results. This can be very useful in cases when you are running a search which is quite broad, or when you are not certain of the best terms to use. When you run searches *AltaVista* will sometimes also provide you with a list of "related searches," which may sometimes prove to be a better search than the one you originally ran.

Refining searches using switches

AltaVista has a number of switches which can be used in combination with single terms or phrase searches to sharpen the search and to narrow it down further. These all take the format <option>:<search string>, and a list of them is included below, with examples:

anchor:text	for hypertext links *anchor:titanic* would find Web pages which use the word "titanic" as a hypertext link

HINTS AND TIPS

Not all search engines allow you to run a phrase search, so check on their help screens, but if they do, you will almost always get a smaller, more focused set of results.

DID YOU KNOW?
According to AltaVista, there are more than twice as many Websites about sex as there are about religion (18,493,992 as against 7,376,505).

applet:class	for finding pages which use certain named Java applets
	applet:fred would find any Web pages which used an applet of class fred
domain:domainname	such as uk, de, jp and so on
	domain:uk would limit results to just those pages with **.uk** in the domain part of the address
host:name	for pages hosted at a site with a particular host name
	host:philb would return sites such as **www.philb.com**
image:filename	for images with specific filenames
	image:clinton.gif would limit the search to pages which contained a gif image with the filename clinton.gif
link:URLtext	for pages which link to the named URL
	link:philb.com would give a list of Web pages which contained links to my site
text:text	for words in the page text
	text:widgets would return pages which had the word "widgets" somewhere within the text of the page
title:text	for words in the title field of a Web page
	title:library would return Web pages which had the word "library" in the title
url:text	for pages with certain words or phrases in the URL
	url:microsoft would find Web pages that contained the word "microsoft" somewhere within the URL.

Of these perhaps the most useful are those to limit your search to specific countries (a full list of the two-letter abbreviations for countries is included in Appendix 2) or within the URL of the Web page. By limiting your search by country you will exclude references to the rest of the world. This is an option which should be used with care, of course – there is no reason why someone in the USA should not publish a page about the English Civil War, for example, and by limiting your search to just UK pages you may be missing out on some potentially valuable information.

However, if your initial search does produce too many possible matches for you, it can be a productive approach, particularly if you are looking for pages which refer to a particular place or region. There are many locations called "Essex," for example, and even limiting that to "Essex County" does not stop references coming up to Essex County in the USA, or alternatively to the County of Essex in the UK if you're particularly interested in just those in the USA. A search strategy which looks like '+*"Essex County"* +*domain:uk*' will overcome that problem. (If you're interested in Essex County in the USA simply replace the '+' in front of *domain:uk* with a '-' to exclude British references.)

This search strategy does, however, have some other limits, particularly if you are looking for commercial companies. Many UK-based companies use the convention of having a URL in the form **http://www.mycompany.co.uk**, but this is just a convention; it is not a requirement. My own URL is **http://www.philb.com**, for example, which gives you no indication at all as to where I am based, or indeed what the subject content of my Website happens to be. Consequently, if you use the domain switch to reduce the number of pages you retrieve, be aware that you may be excluding valuable information.

The option of choosing to search in the URL may be worth considering, since it will simply return a list of pages which include the word or phrase you have asked for within their URL. A search for url:library would return pages such as: http://www.philb.com/library.htm and http://www.libraryland.org. However, it would not give you pages which included the word "libraries" in the URL or the word "library" in the main body of the text. Nonetheless, it is reasonably safe to assume that a good Web page designer is going to create pages named in such a way as to reflect their content.

Focusing a search

Let's start to put some of these things into practice and see how we can reduce the number of hits which *AltaVista* offers us. The following searches were run in 2001, so you'll get different results if you run the searches yourself, but they should

DID YOU KNOW?
My site is actually based in Manchester England, just in case you were wondering!

DID YOU KNOW?

When this search was included in the first edition, the result was 494,138 hits – an increase of 7,186,006 pages in just over three years!

Fig. 3.2 *Partial results from an "AltaVista" search*
© 2001 AltaVista Company

illustrate the point.

'*Jaguar car cars automobile automobiles vehicle vehicles*' produced a total of 7,662,144 hits.
'Jaguar car cars automobile automobiles vehicle vehicles -animal -cat' reduced this to a total of 3,528.
"Jaguar cars" as a phrase search gives us 39,360 references.
'+"Jaguar cars" +domain:uk' further reduced this to 1,608 hits.
'*+url:Jaguar +domain:uk*' gave a more workable number of 945 hits.

You will of course get different results with different combinations of the syntax, but the examples above should give you some ideas of how to proceed with your own searches.

Viewing results

Once you have run your search, *AltaVista* will display the results on the screen for you to look at. I've reproduced a sample screen in Figure 3.2.

The first line gives you the title of the page (as defined by the Web-page author), followed by its URL. Then you see a brief summary of the page, which is taken either from the first few words that *AltaVista* finds, or from a special "meta" tag used when designing pages. Beneath that you see the option to translate this information into another language, which is discussed in more detail in a moment. There will also be an option to view more pages from the particular site, which can be useful if you need to get a better overview of a particular site, and also an option for related pages. This will tell *AltaVista* to locate other pages from different sites that have similar content. You can do this manually if you prefer by using the syntax *like:url_of_website*, such as *like:http://www.philb.com/*.

If you wish to go directly to one of the Web pages, you can click on the title element, and your Web browser will cut the link with *AltaVista* and take you to the selected site.

The example in Figure 3.2 only has a few results, but in most cases you will find a number of hits displayed on the screen for you, with more available on subsequent pages. The first ten references are displayed on the screen, and you can move to the next page by simply clicking "next" on the button bar at the bottom of the page, or by choosing a specific page of results to view. In most cases, there will be little point in going beyond the first couple of pages of results; either because you have found the information that you need, or because your search was not as focused as it might have been; if you're still turning up appropriate pages after you've looked at 20 or 30 sites, you should re-run the search, making it tighter.

Real names and keywords

Before we move on, there is just one other rather interesting feature in *AltaVista* that I'd like to draw your attention to. If you take another look at Figure 3.2, at the top of the screen you will see a link to a particular word or phrase (in our example "Jaguar cars") followed by the legend "Click on this Internet keyword to go directly to the Jaguar cars Website." This is known as a "keyword," and is quickly becoming a popular way to search the Internet. The service is provided by a company called Real Names (their Website is at **http://web.realnames.com/**) and their aim is to provide

HINTS AND TIPS

AltaVista will search for pages in any one of 25 languages, from Chinese to Swedish.

Fig. 3.3 *"AltaVista" advanced search screen*
© 2001 AltaVista Company

easier access to Websites without having to remember cumbersome addresses. A company can purchase a keyword from Real Names for an annual fee and they may also pay extra if users actually click on the link to go directly to their site. Consequently it can be a very useful way of getting quickly to exactly the site that you're interested in, and while not a foolproof method, may save you considerable time. Incidentally, it is a system that also allows users to input a keyword directly into the location box of their browser if it is a keyword-enabled browser such as Microsoft Internet Explorer 4.x or higher and you will be instantly delivered to the Web page of the organization that has purchased the use of that name.

Searching *AltaVista*: advanced search

If you take another look at Figure 3.1 you will see that there is an option in the bottom right hand corner for an advanced search. Even if you are an experienced searcher, I would suggest that you spend some time with the easy search screen to begin with, just to get a feel for the way the search engine works. When you decide to move on to the advanced features, you will see a screen which looks something like Figure 3.3.

As you can see, the search element of the screen does not appear substantially different from the easy search version, with the exception of a Boolean expression input field and a pair of date boxes. You should consider using the advanced search screen once you have become familiar with the general search process, or when you have a very specific query in mind. Most searches can be run perfectly well using the simple form, but the major disadvantage of it is of course that *AltaVista* controls the relevance-ranking process. In the advanced format you have more control over how words or phrases are ranked, Boolean operators can be used to greater effect, and you have control over the date field.

Another difference will become apparent as soon as you attempt to run a search, which is that the '+' and '-' switches do not work – you must use Boolean operators, and they should be in upper case. *AltaVista* gives you an alternative here, however, and allows you to use the characters & for AND, | for OR, ! for NOT, and ~ for NEAR.

The date range allows you just to retrieve pages which were updated during a particular period of time, using the dd/mm/yy format. This can be very useful if you wish to run a search on a regular basis to retrieve just those documents added or modified since the last time you ran the search. (If you do not enter a date, *AltaVista* defaults to the current year, which means that you may get a rather odd result if you are searching on 2 January!)

The 'sort by:' box (the unlabelled single-line input field) is also very important – if you do not use it, *AltaVista* will not rank the results which it retrieves for you, and you will be likely to end up with an unusable set of results. You can either re-enter some of the terms that you have already entered in the Boolean expression box, or you can add more terms which further define your search. To continue with the automobile example from earlier in this chapter, we might decide to run a search for "*Jaguar AND cars*" and rank the results using the terms "*renovation*" and "*restoration.*"

The advanced search facilities also allow you to make use of parentheses ( ) in a manner similar to that which you might have experienced if you have used any online or CD-

ROM-based search engines. The *AltaVista* help pages give a nice example here which is worth repeating: '*president AND ((George NEAR Bush) AND ((Bill OR William) NEAR Clinton))*'.

You will also notice from the previous example that *AltaVista* allows you to make use of the NEAR operator, and there are times when this will be more effective than doing a phrase search. For example, if you wanted to do a search for cattle breeding and did a phrase search for "*cattle breeding*," that is exactly what you would get. You would therefore potentially miss any references to "breeding cattle" or "cattle; problems associated with breeding." The NEAR operator overcomes this problem, since it will find Web pages on which the two terms appear, in either order, within ten words of each other, so in this case a better search would be "*cattle NEAR breeding.*" Unfortunately it is not possible (at the time of writing) to define the number of words between the two keywords that counts as 'NEAR' – *AltaVista* predefines this as up to ten words.

A final useful switch which *AltaVista* has available is the wildcard function. This allows you to broaden out your search to include plurals, or anything which starts with a given sequence of characters. For example, if you want to start by doing a broad search for anything to do with libraries, you could try '*librar**', which will retrieve a set of records including library, libraries, librarianship, librarian and so on. The disadvantage of this approach is that you may retrieve a huge number of hits, so you should use it with caution, or right at the end of the word, just to catch a plural ending. (This option is also available in the Easy Search mode.)

Searching *AltaVista*: other facilities

We have so far covered both basic and advanced search features, concentrating on the advantages and disadvantages of the available syntax. However, *AltaVista* also allows you rather more flexibility than that, and if you once more refer to Figure 3.1 you'll begin to see an indication of some of the other options that are available.

For example, you may choose to search in a particular language. This feature was introduced into *AltaVista* in July

1997. It allows you to limit a search to just a single language, which at first sight doesn't appear to be particularly valuable. After all, if you include a foreign-language word you would expect that the vast majority of pages which you turn up are going to be in that particular language. However, if your first language is something other than English the value of the option becomes much clearer, since using it will eliminate any English pages, allowing you to work with a smaller, more focused set of results. *AltaVista* is able to do this because it employs dictionary-based algorithms to work out the language of the page; as a result, pages which are written predominately in English, but which include one or two foreign words, are correctly classified as English.

If you do find a foreign-language page which looks interesting, but you are unable to understand the language in question, all is not lost, since AltaVista introduced another new feature at the end of 1997, allowing you to translate pages into and from a variety of different languages. I've used this a few times, and while the translation is not perfect (and does sometimes include some of the howlers that computer-generated translations create!) it is usually enough to get by with.

I'd next like to draw your attention to the other options available under the search box, which I've reproduced in Figure 3.4.

There are a number of "shopping" options which allow you to compare prices, look for local deals and auctions. Since these are probably not of particular interest to the majority of information professionals (at least not in a work environment!), I'll leave you to explore those by yourself; I'm sure

---

Try your search in: Shopping · Images · Video · MP3/Audio · News · Autos · Tech · Real Estate

Search for: Help | Customize Settings | Family Filter is **off**

[   ] [any language ▼] [Search]

Text-Only Search | Search Assistant | Advanced Search

Shopping: Compare Prices · Back to School Store · Sales & Rebates · Bid & Win

Tools: E-mail · Translate · Maps · Yellow Pages · People Finder · Find a Date
Find Downloads · Weight Calculator · Find a Job · Find a Home · Plan a Trip

News: Scientists Say Frenzy Over Shark Attacks Is... *New York Times* · More News...

Fig. 3.4   *Other "AltaVista" search options*
© 2001 AltaVista Company

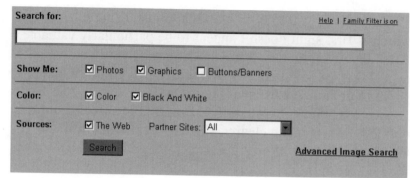

Fig. 3.5   *Image searching on "AltaVista"*
© 2001 AltaVista Company

you can work out what they do. Below these options are a
number of other quite powerful search tools such as Image
Search, Maps, Yellow Pages, and People Finder.

Image Search is exactly what you would imagine – it
allows you to search for particular images, and an example of
the search screen at this point is shown in Figure 3.5. You
can run a search just as you would in the search mode, but
rather than locate Web pages, *AltaVista* will try and find specific images for you. Since I'll be talking about finding
images in Chapter 7 I'll delay further discussion until that
point.

Maps and Directions are specific to the USA, but they
allow you to input a particular address and see a map on the
screen of the place you are interested in, with the option of
zooming in or out to view the map at a different magnifica-
tion. Unsurprisingly, Directions allows you to input two
addresses in the USA and to receive a series of instructions
on how to drive from point A to point B.

The Yellow Pages option is specific to the USA and
Canada, and provides you with a quick and easy way to
locate, for example, florists in Richmond, Virginia.

The People Finder is the equivalent of the White Pages
(again for the USA and Canada) and allows you to locate a
named individual, so if you happen to know that your friend
Robert E. Lee lives in Richmond, Virginia, it should be
quite possible to trace him.

Finally, there is also an option entitled Breaking News. In
common with many other search engines, *AltaVista* can provide you with current news events and stories in 13 different

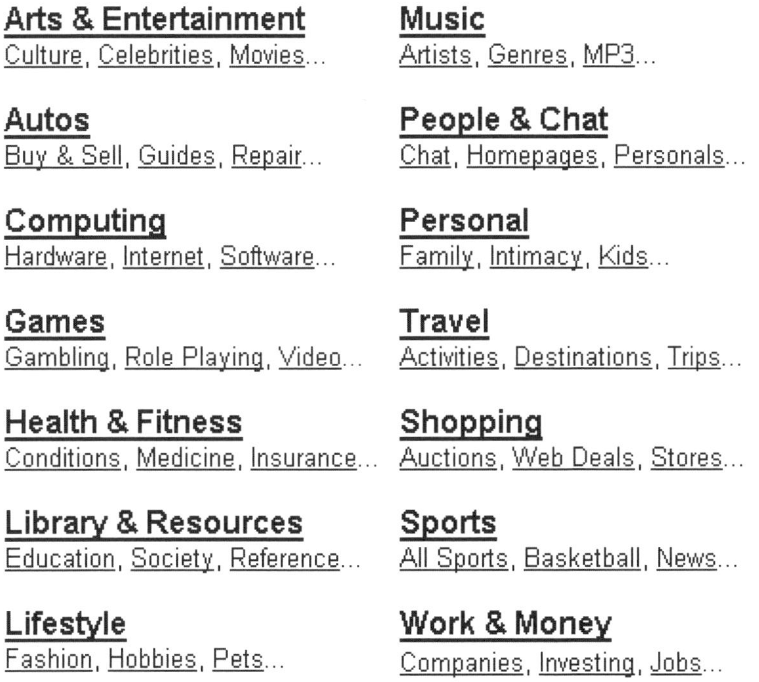

Arts & Entertainment
Culture, Celebrities, Movies...

Music
Artists, Genres, MP3...

Autos
Buy & Sell, Guides, Repair...

People & Chat
Chat, Homepages, Personals...

Computing
Hardware, Internet, Software...

Personal
Family, Intimacy, Kids...

Games
Gambling, Role Playing, Video...

Travel
Activities, Destinations, Trips...

Health & Fitness
Conditions, Medicine, Insurance...

Shopping
Auctions, Web Deals, Stores...

Library & Resources
Education, Society, Reference...

Sports
All Sports, Basketball, News...

Lifestyle
Fashion, Hobbies, Pets...

Work & Money
Companies, Investing, Jobs...

Fig. 3.6 *Major headings and subheadings for the "AltaVista" direc-*
tory
© 2001 AltaVista Company

categories from Asia–Pacific to Technical News from a wide
variety of news sources such as the BBC, CNN, the
International Herald Tribune and so on.

Below these sections you will see a directory listing of subjects. *AltaVista* began life as a straightforward free-text search
engine, but has since added another way to search the
Internet. You can see the directory structure in Figure 3.6, and
the concept behind it is quite simple – just identify the
appropriate category, choose a subheading, then perhaps
another one to further focus your search, click on the appropriate Website link and visit the site. The directory currently
has over 2,000,000 Web pages, which have been chosen by
human editors for their appropriateness and relevance in any
particular category. Consequently it is a quick and simple
approach to finding information, although it does not have as
many headings, subheadings or listings as index/directory
search engines such as *Yahoo!*.

In the last year or so *AltaVista* has started to add regional
variants of the search engine, so it is now possible to search 30

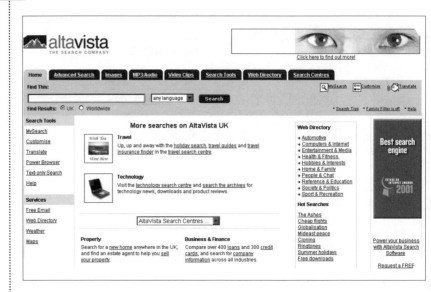

Fig. 3.7   *The UK "AltaVista" main page, showing the search interface*
© 2001 AltaVista Company

regional versions of the search engine. The UK variant can be found at **http://uk.altavista.com/** and although the interface does look rather different (as you can see from Figure 3.7) the functionality is almost exactly the same. The major difference is that the search engine will default to finding Web pages from the particular country concerned, although you can if you wish ask it to search the entire Web instead.

Lycos

Established in May 1994, *Lycos* at **http://www.lycos.com** is one of the oldest of the search engines, and began as a project at the Carnegie Mellon University. *Lycos* used to be just a straightforward free-text search engine, allowing you to input any terms you wished in order to locate appropriate Websites, but in common with other free-text search engines it now also provides a directory listing of sites in a hierarchy. Topics in the *Lycos* hierarchy operate in a similar fashion to the directory outlined in *AltaVista*.

Figure 3.8 shows the opening *Lycos* search screen, which easily and quickly allows you to type in the words or phrases you want to find. An advanced search function allows you to search for all the words, any of the words or the exact phrase and to further refine the search by choosing specific types of

DID YOU KNOW?
Lycos comes from the Latin for "wolf spider."

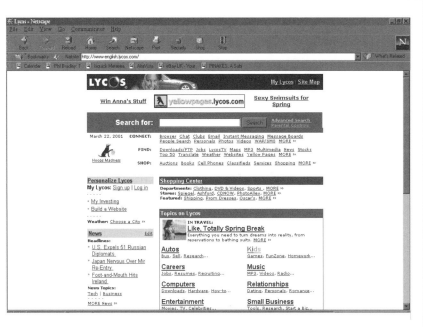

Fig. 3.8 *The "Lycos" simple search screen*
© 2001 Lycos Inc.

documents such as home pages. It is also possible to run more complex searches, although it is not necessarily immediately apparent how that is to be achieved. However, if you refer to Figure 3.9, you will see that on the left hand side of the screen are several other options – Page Field, Language, Link Referrals – which allow you to narrow to words in the title, or the URL, or choose from 25 different languages. It is, however, important to note that this advanced search functionality differs if you use it on the local versions of

HINTS AND TIPS

Always check to see if a search engine offers help screens – not all do, but they can be very useful and provide valuable tips on search techniques.

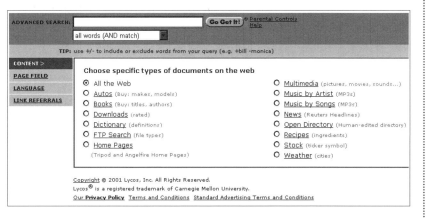

Fig. 3.9 *An example of the "Lycos" advanced search functions*
© 2001 Lycos Inc.

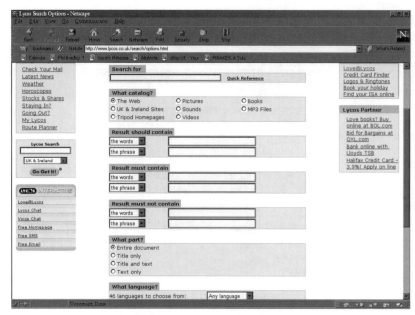

Fig. 3.10 *"Lycos" advanced search interface*
© 2001 Lycos Inc.

Lycos, and Figure 3.10 shows you the advanced interface for the UK version of the search engine. If, as a searcher, you are happier with a command line type interface *Lycos* does support a number of Boolean operators. Using these you can incorporate Boolean operators directly into your searches, and the search engine also has powerful facilities for adjacency searching. Features offered include the following operators:

➤ ADJ – club ADJ football retrieves sites which contain both words next to each other in any order.
➤ NEAR – football NEAR club retrieves sites where both terms are within 25 words of each other in any order.
➤ FAR – club FAR football retrieves sites which contain both words more than 25 words apart.
➤ BEFORE – football BEFORE club is the same as the AND operator, but the first word must come before the second word, any distance apart.

It is also possible to specify the order of words by including O (for order) immediately before the operator:

➤ OADJ – football OADJ club is equivalent to searching for "football club."

➤ ONEAR – football ONEAR club retrieves sites where the terms are within 25 words of each other and football comes first.

➤ OFAR – is like ONEAR except that the terms must be more than 25 words apart.

If the default of 25 words separating terms is not appropriate, this can be changed by adding a forward slash and the number of words immediately after it, such as football NEAR/5 club.

Naturally, these operators can all be combined, leading to very powerful search structures.

In common with other search engines, *Lycos* has added new features in order to increase its popularity; it offers e-mail services, chat rooms, a personalized news service, free SMS, home page and so on.

HotBot

HotBot is a search engine that was created by Wired Ventures Inc. – the same organization that publishes *Wired* magazine; it can be found at **http://www.hotbot.com**. In common with other search engines, *HotBot* provides both easy and advanced interfaces; part of the advanced interface is shown in Figure 3.11.

The simple search allows you to search for all words, any words, the exact phrase, or links to a URL. You can also specify if the page should contain an image, MP3 file, video, audio or PDF files. HotBot also provides a "browse by category" option, which has the look and feel of the AltaVista approach, with major categories such as "Business and Finance," "Travel and Vacation" and so on. Once you click on one of these categories, they are then subdivided into more specific sections, and so on. HotBot has links to search for other types of information, such as Usenet, Yellow and White Pages (US only), e-mail addresses, domain names, classified adverts, top news sites, homes and loans, stocks and shareware.

The advanced search facility is very flexible, with considerable functionality. Searchers can use all of the options previously described, and also limit the search by date, domain or location (including continents, rather than just by individual countries). One particularly nice feature is the ability to

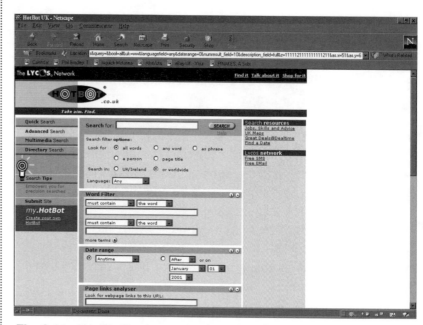

Fig. 3.11 *"HotBot" advanced search features*

limit searches to pages which include certain types of media, such as sound files or video. This is very useful if you need to look for information in a variety of formats – you could, for example, search for sites referring to the moon landings, and by limiting this to sound and video sites you could retrieve pages that include transmissions of conversations between NASA and the astronauts as well as video footage of them engaged in moonwalks.

Northern Light

Northern Light (**http://www.northernlight.com**), while not a new search engine (it was briefly mentioned in the first edition), has over a very short period of time become one of the major players in the search engine market. It was established in 1995 and has grown consistently since then, currently indexing over 315 million Web pages.

The simple search interface, in common with other search engines, allows you to input single terms or a number of terms, to do phrase searching and to use Boolean operators. It also supports the use of right-side truncation, truncation inside a word (using the asterisk), or single-letter replacement using the percentage symbol. Consequently, you can search for:

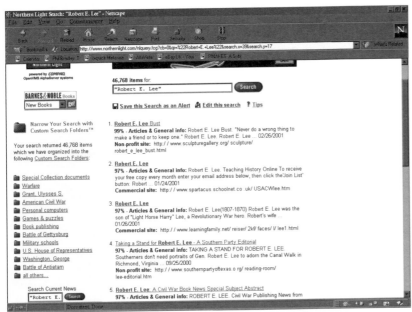

Fig. 3.12 *Custom search folder in "Northern Light"*
© 1997–2001 Northern Light Technology Inc.

➤ librar* – which will result in pages that contain words that begin with "librar" such as library, librarian, librarianship

➤ psych*ist – which will find all results which contain words that begin with "psych" and end with "ist" (e.g. psychologist, psychiatrist)

➤ gene%logy – which will return sites containing words beginning with "gene" and ending with "logy," separated by a single letter (e.g. genealogy and geneology); this can be useful for commonly misspelled words.

Field searches can also be run, to find words in the title or the URL (by the use of *title:* and *url:*), or for a particular company (using *company:*). A particularly nice feature allows the results to be sorted by date, from newest to oldest, by using the command *sort:date*.

Consequently, *Northern Light* is a very flexible search engine, offering a high level of functionality. However, it does not end there. Once you have run a search, *Northern Light* will return Web pages that match the criteria you have asked for, but it also creates a series of custom search folders, as can be seen in Figure 3.12. The search was for the American Civil

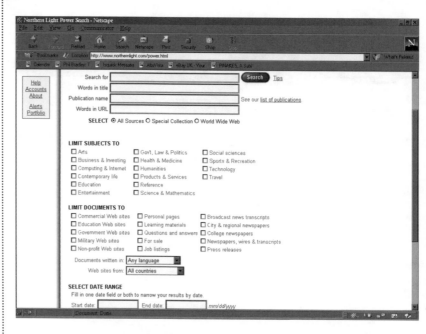

Fig. 3.13 *"Northern Light" and its advanced search function*
© 1997–2001 Northern Light Technology Inc.

War general Robert E. Lee, and the search engine has
returned over 46,000 results. Normally it would be necessary
to refine the search, but the custom search folders provide the
searcher with the opportunity to focus on particular subject
areas such as the American Civil War, particular battles, military schools and so on. Consequently, if we had an interest in
his role in the Battle of Gettysburg, then by clicking on the
custom search folder for that entry we can immediately
reduce our search results to just over 600. Moreover, we now
have another series of search folders, giving us the opportunity
of narrowing down the search even further.

These custom search folders are uniquely created for each
search that is run, based on the content of the Web pages that
Northern Light finds. They are therefore a very useful way of
narrowing down a search, even if you have very little knowledge or information about the subject that you are looking for.

It is also worth briefly mentioning the information contained in each result as it is returned by *Northern Light*. In
many instances other search engines give a fairly limited
amount of information about the particular Web page – often
just a few words of summary – but with this search engine, as
well as the title of the Web page, there is an indication of how

relevant *Northern Light* considers the page to be in the light of the search which was run, the date of the Web page, and the type of site the page is from, such as a commercial site, an educational site and so on.

As you would expect, *Northern Light* has an advanced search function, which can be seen in Figure 3.13. The advanced search functionality allows the user to search in title, URL and so on as you would expect, but it also has functionality to limit to particular subjects (such as business or reference), to particular types of site (such as government Websites) to Websites from particular countries or specific languages (although it only provides support for five languages), or to specific date ranges; the results can be sorted in order of date or relevance.

Another important element of the *Northern Light* service is their Special Collection. This is a collection of full-text articles from over 7000 journals, books, magazines, newswires and reference sources. These can be viewed by clicking on the custom search folder for the special collection, or in the advanced search facility the search can be limited to the special collection rather than the whole of the Web. A summary of the results can be viewed, together with bibliographic information about each article, and these can be ordered online if it is necessary to view the entire document. The majority of prices are between $2 and $5, although some may be more expensive, depending on the document. Not only is this a useful periodical resource, it allows you to keep up to date with articles published in particular areas of interest, and if you don't have access to the specific journal yourself, the article can be obtained almost instantly.

Other free-text search engines

There is almost no limit to the number of free-text search engines that are available, and it would be quite possible to write an entire book on them, rather than just a single chapter. If you do not feel inspired to use any of those that I have already listed, you may wish to explore some others for yourself, and I have listed some URLs below to get you started. It should not be regarded as a complete list, however.

AOL Anywhere:	**http://search.aol.com**
Espotting:	**http://www.espotting.com**
EuroSeek:	**http://www.euroseek.com**
Google:	**http://www.google.com**
Look Smart:	**http://www.looksmart.com**
SearchEurope:	**http://www.searcheurope.com**
Webcrawler:	**http://www.webcrawler.com**

Summary

In this chapter I have gone into detail about how to use free-text search engines, using *AltaVista* as my major example. Almost all free-text search engines are now offering some sort of directory approach as well, but their major strength lies in their ability to translate free-text terms into a meaningful search, and to return a list of results based on a relevance-ranked approach.

Some of them are more sophisticated than others, and the advanced search facilities are constantly improving. Given this rate of improvement, it should not take very much longer before they offer the type of search techniques which online and CD-ROM systems have been offering for many years.

URLs mentioned in this chapter

http://www.altavista.com
http://www.philb.com
http://www.libraryland.org
http://web.realnames.com/
http://uk.altavista.com
http://www.lycos.com
http://www.hotbot.com
http://search.aol.com
http://www.espotting.com
http://www.euroseek.com
http://www.google.com
http://www.looksmart.com
http://www.searcheurope.com
http://www.webcrawler.com
http://www.northernlight.com

4

Index-based search engines

Introduction

Free-text search engines are just one way of finding the information that you need on the Internet. They are very good if you know exactly what you are looking for and can identify it using a small number of keywords or phrases. However, they are less useful if you require a broad overview of a subject, or if you are unfamiliar with a subject and its technical jargon. This is where index-based search engines are much more appropriate.

Index-based search engines:

➤ arrange data in a structured fashion
➤ make use of headings and subheadings going from the general to the specific
➤ usually rely on Web authors to submit pages to the engine
➤ depend on their category structure for their success
➤ are generally quite simple to use, and appeal to novice searchers
➤ are useful if you want a broad approach to a subject
➤ are useful if you are unsure of what keywords to use in a search.

Yahoo!

The first index-based search engine which I'll look at in detail is *Yahoo!*, which was started in 1994 by two students at Stanford University, David Filo and Jerry Yang. It can be found at **http://www.yahoo.com**. It started when the two decided that they needed some sensible way of keeping track of their interests on the Web, rather than continuing to use their own large and cumbersome lists of Websites. They

DID YOU KNOW?
YAHOO! stands for Yet Another Hierarchical Officious Oracle.

developed software to allow them to quickly locate, identify and edit materials, and over the course of time *Yahoo!* has evolved into a highly effective and valuable search engine.

This list-based approach is still quite obvious when you look at *Yahoo!*. Figure 4.1 is taken from the *Yahoo!* front page, showing the top-level subject headings. These are:

➤ arts and humanities
➤ business and economy
➤ computers and Internet
➤ education
➤ entertainment
➤ government
➤ health
➤ news and media
➤ recreation and sports
➤ reference
➤ regional
➤ science
➤ social science
➤ society and culture.

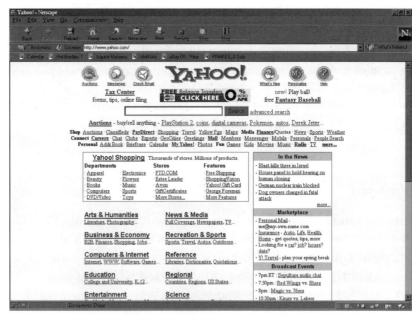

Fig. 4.1   *The "Yahoo!" front page*
© 2001 Yahoo! Inc.

Below these 14 major headings there are another 47 second-level headings, and so on.

You can already see a major difference in the approach taken by *Yahoo!* (and indeed other index-based search engines) in that you can immediately see the type of information which is available. With a free-text search engine it is necessary to run a search before being in a position to see the data the engine covers.

Human indexing rather than computer generation

A second major difference is that all of these headings and subheadings have been created by people; there is a much greater human input into index-based search engines than you will normally find with free-text engines. This is both an advantage and a disadvantage. The advantage is that it is easier to work out the way in which another human being thinks than it is to second-guess a computer, so if you think of a subject, you can probably guess with a reasonable level of accuracy which of the major subject headings will cover that subject. The disadvantage is paradoxically the same: the success of an index-based approach depends on the user thinking in the same way that the creator of the index does. If the creator of the index has a different bias (cultural or geographical, for example) you may spend a long time searching for your information in entirely the wrong place. I will go into this in more detail later in the chapter.

However, for now, let's look into *Yahoo!* in rather more detail. Clicking on any of the subheadings brings up another page, which provides you with a further breakdown of the subject, and so on, until you finally reach a page which gives you a list of sites that you can click on. Figure 4.2 illustrates what happens when you click on the top-level heading "Reference." The numbers in brackets after each subheading indicate the total number of Websites listed under that heading, and the @ sign indicates that the heading is also used elsewhere within the index, so it is possible to move between different subjects easily in order to find the information which you require. This is particularly the case with commercial categories, which are linked to their appropriate non-commercial counterparts.

DID YOU KNOW?
The use of the @ symbol in e-mails originated with Ray Tomlinson, an engineer with an acoustic engineering company. The content of the first e-mail he sent has been forgotten.
(http://www.forbes. com/asap/1998/1005/ 126.html)

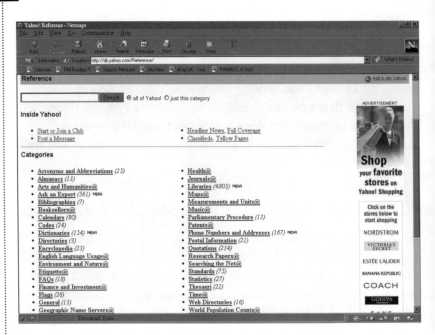

Fig. 4.2 *"Yahoo!" subheadings below the top-level "Reference" heading*
© 2001 Yahoo! Inc.

This last point is an important one with respect to *Yahoo!*. When authors register their page(s) with the search engine, they can choose up to two categories within which to list the page, and if it is a commercial site, it must be placed under a commercial section. You should take this into account when using the engine. To use the example given by *Yahoo!*, if you have an interest in baseball cards, sites which cover this subject can be found in two places:

➤ Business and Economy: Companies: Sports: Collectibles: Cards: Baseball
➤ Recreation: Sports: Baseball: Collectibles: Baseball Cards: Commercial@

and these two categories are linked.

This also works for regions of the world, and is an area that can cause some confusion. If you have an interest in the British General Election of 1997, the most sensible place to begin your search may at first glance appear to be under the Government: Politics hierarchy. However, because this is specific to a single region (i.e. the United Kingdom), it is necessary to look under the Regional heading – Regional:

Countries: United_Kingdom: Government: Politics: Elections: 1997_General_Election. The Government: Politics hierarchy immediately takes you into information on the American political system.

If a Website is in any way regional, *Yahoo!* will always place it in the appropriate regional category, rather than directly into a main subject category, and the only time this rule is superseded is when a subject or an organization is global in nature. In most cases you will need to remember to check under the appropriate regional heading, although in most instances *Yahoo!* will also cross-reference directly to the subject area as well.

The basic approach to using *Yahoo!* is therefore quite simple: decide which major heading your subject comes under, and follow the links through the hierarchy until you reach it. As a result of this simplicity it is a very good search engine to direct novice searchers towards, and as long as they are made aware of some of the idiosyncrasies of the system they should be able to retrieve good results quickly.

Advanced searching in *Yahoo!*

If you refer back to Figure 4.1 you will notice that there is a search box, which sits above the subject listing. This can be used to save a lot of time, as some of the hierarchies are quite deep (the general election example above goes down seven levels, for example) and it can be quite a time-consuming task to click on a heading, wait for the page to load, click on the next and so on. A faster and more effective approach is to make use of the search box. You can input your search here, and *Yahoo!* will present you with five sets of responses:

➤ category names
➤ Website titles
➤ Web pages
➤ *Yahoo!* news stories
➤ *Yahoo!* shopping.

This is very useful for a number of reasons:

➤ The returned list of categories allows you to identify quickly

```
+diabetes -children          Search   advanced search
```

Fig. 4.3   *Using the search option in "Yahoo!" to look for diabetes, but not children*

the precise section of the hierarchy which is appropriate.

➤ You can go directly to the category without going through the process of clicking on a seemingly endless series of headings.

➤ The whole process can be circumnavigated by going directly to one of the Websites listed.

➤ If your interest is in current affairs the section on related news may provide you with up-to-the-minute information.

Figure 4.3 gives an example of how this works in practice, when I did a search on diabetes, but which excluded children. Figure 4.4 is a portion of the results which were returned to me.

You can see from the search that I made use of the + symbol to include the particular word that I wanted, together with the – symbol to exclude references to children (of

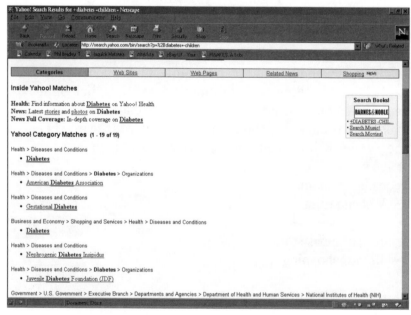

Fig. 4.4   *Partial results of the diabetes search*
© 2001 Yahoo! Inc.

course, if I had been doing a proper search I would also have excluded references to child and juvenile, but this search was just for demonstration purposes). *Yahoo!* includes some of the common operator symbols, such as we have already seen in operation at *AltaVista*, but it also has some others, such as t:<text> to search in the title of a document, or u:<text> to search in a URL. *Yahoo!* also allows phrase searching with double quotes (" "), and wildcard matching using the * symbol. Next to the search box is a link to the advanced search function, allowing you to limit to an exact phrase, search *Yahoo!* categories or Websites, or new listings.

When *Yahoo!* does a search of this type, it searches through the four areas of its database as mentioned previously. If *Yahoo!* is unable to find any sites or categories that match the search, it will automatically pass on the search request to *Google* and return any results. It therefore makes sense to make use of the syntax which *Google* understands, in order to get a tightly focused set of results.

In the diabetes example, I was returned a total of 19 categories and 317 Websites that matched my criteria, which therefore enabled me to decide quickly where to go next. In many ways this is a more helpful approach than we find with free-text search engines if you know little about the subject, since the categories returned give you a very clear idea of what is actually available within that general subject area.

Yahoo! ranks the Web pages it finds using its own set of algorithms:

➤ Multiple keywords. Any document which contains all of your keywords is ranked higher than one which contains fewer of them.
➤ Title words. Any words found in the title are weighted as being more important than those which only occur in the body of the text or in the URL.
➤ Category. More general category matches are placed before more specific matches.

HINTS AND TIPS

Search engines rank their results according to their own criteria, so the same search will result in a different set of results on different search engines.

Yahoo! does, however, go further than this, since you can also do a search within a specific subject area. There are times when you may be quite clear on the particular approach you wish to take to a specific subject, but even when the search

Fig. 4.5   *A subject-specific search in a "Yahoo!" category*
© 2001 Yahoo! Inc.

has been narrowed down using the hierarchical structure there may still be many hundreds or indeed thousands of Websites available. It is possible to limit a *Yahoo!* search to a specific category; when you navigate through the hierarchy, *Yahoo!* always displays a search box similar to the one we have already seen in Figure 4.3, but it includes an option to search just within the current category, as Figure 4.5 illustrates.

An interest in the Star Trek spacecraft *USS Enterprise* will, in all probability, give me far too many hits if I do a general search in *Yahoo!*, but by narrowing myself down into the News and Media: Television: Genres: Science fiction, fantasy and horror: Star Trek section, a search just within this category will substantially reduce the number of results and will automatically focus on that one area, instead of finding everything on the subject.

As you can see, *Yahoo!* is not a difficult search engine to use; in fact it is very straightforward. However, the value in using it does not only rest on its simplicity, but also on the fact that it has a number of other very useful features as well. *Yahoo!*, in common with other major search engines, is always attempting to broaden its user base, and as a result has a regular program of updating and adding new features. Some of these have little relevance to us as searchers, but others can prove quite useful. If you return to look at Figure 4.5 for a moment you will see that there are a number of icons at the top of the screen, and below the search box is another series of links. I'll briefly go through these features, and highlight those which have particular value to searchers.

➤ *Auctions*. *Yahoo!* runs an auction site, which allows users to buy and sell items in an auction environment. Although there is little direct use as far as searchers are concerned (unless of course you are seeking prices for various items) it can sometimes be useful if you are looking to purchase items for specific collections.

➤ *Messenger*. This is a messaging service which allows users to chat in real time to other users of the system.

➤ *Check Email*. Again, related specifically to *Yahoo!* users who have a *Yahoo!* e-mail account.

➤ *What's New*. This can sometimes be worth a quick look, if only to keep up to date with any changes that are being made to the search engine. You can choose to look in any of the major categories to see which new sites they have added.

➤ *Personalize*. This allows you to personalize the information that you receive from *Yahoo!* and to create your own pages of information. This aspect of the *Yahoo!* service is discussed later in Chapter 11.

➤ *Help*. A set of very useful and comprehensive help screens; if you get stuck, this is certainly the place to start looking!

➤ *Shop*. As can be seen from Figure 4.5, this section includes sections on auctions, classified advertisements, shopping and so on. Of particular interest to searchers are the sections on Yellow Pages and maps. These allow you to search for companies who specialize in particular areas, or to display maps of particular areas and driving instructions on how to reach them.

➤ *Media*. This section provides information on investing, personal finance, business news, world finance and summary information. Similar information is also available for news, sports and the weather.

➤ *Connect*. Search for new jobs, chat to friends and colleagues, find experts in particular subject areas (which can also be useful if you're really stuck and cannot find an answer to a specific question anywhere else; one of the *Yahoo!* experts may well be able to assist you). You can also search for individuals (covered later in more detail in Chapter 8) and so on.

➤ *Personal*. This allows users to set up their own address books, calendars and so on.

➤ *Fun*. I think I can safely say that this category is self explanatory!

Regional Yahoo!s

Earlier I mentioned that one problem with *Yahoo!* is that in order to find information on a particular region, it is necessary to drill down through the regional heading to reach the data that you are interested in. *Yahoo!* has approached this problem by providing local *Yahoo!s*. They are continually adding new ones to their service, so there is little point in trying to list those that they currently have; I would simply suggest that you visit *Yahoo!* yourself and view *Local Yahoo!s* or *More Yahoo!s*. I will, however, spend a little time looking at the UK & Ireland version, to illustrate the difference between the main engine and the regional ones. This version can be reached by clicking on the link from the main *Yahoo!* home page, or by going to **http://www.yahoo.co.uk.**

As you can see from a comparison of Figures 4.1 and 4.6, there is very little difference between the two indexes; both have the same physical appearance, and both work in exactly the same way, with broadly the same options. There are some slight differences, however – with the global version, there is a link to *Yahoo! Yellow Pages*, but in the UK & Ireland version you will find a *UK Business Directory* instead.

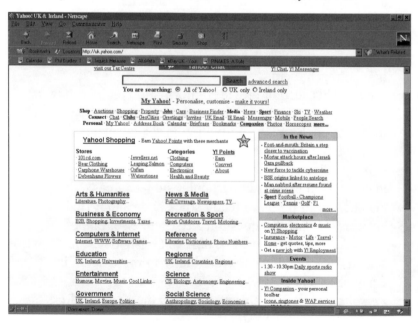

Fig. 4.6   *"UK & Ireland Yahoo!"* home page
© 2001 Yahoo! Inc.

There are some larger differences when you inspect the major subject headings. For example, in the global version we find:

Government
Elections, Military, Law, Taxes

and in the UK & Ireland version we have:

Government
UK, Ireland, Europe, Politics

which does reflect an appropriately different emphasis. The observant searcher will also notice differences when drilling down into the hierarchy. Users of a regional *Yahoo!* can choose to search either the entire database (which is the same as running the search on the global version), or choose to search in the UK categories, for example. This is essentially the same as choosing the appropriate regional category from the global *Yahoo!*, but it is a rather faster route through to the same information. Even if you decide not to follow the UK route, once you have drilled far enough down into the category, the first sites which are displayed will be those which have a regional importance.

This can best be illustrated by looking at the category of *Reference Libraries* in both the global version (Figure 4.7) and the UK & Ireland version (Figure 4.8).

You can see that substantially there is very little difference: both versions have subheadings for Law Libraries@ and Lesbian, Gay and Bisexual@, for example. However, once we look at the sites which are returned in this category, the global version displays a simple alphabetical list of sites, while the UK & Ireland version begins with sites that are appropriate to both countries, indicating this with the use of small flags.

Consequently, there can be particular advantages to searching in a regional version of *Yahoo!*, rather than in the global version:

➤ Subjects appropriate to a region or country can be located more quickly.
➤ It is less confusing for novices to use.
➤ Appropriate Websites are given greater prominence.
➤ Fewer matches are returned.

HINTS AND TIPS
If you want a geographic search, use a local version of *Yahoo!*, but if you want a comprehensive view, make use of the main version.

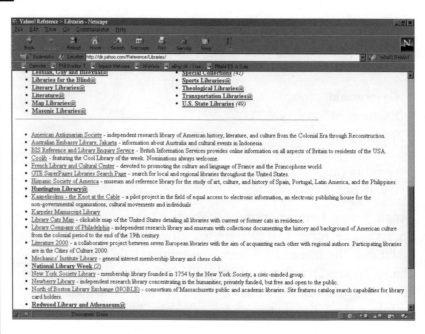

Fig. 4.7 The global "Yahoo!" section for "Reference Libraries,"
including headings and links to Websites

© 2001 Yahoo! Inc.

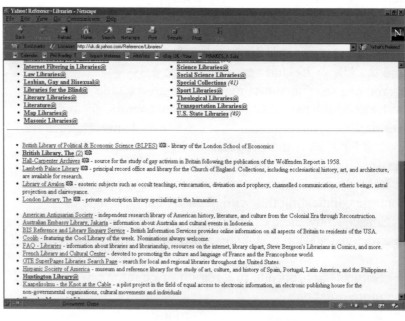

Fig. 4.8 The "UK & Ireland Yahoo!" section for "Reference Libraries,"
including headings and links to Websites

© 2001 Yahoo! Inc.

Yahoo! summary

Yahoo! is not a search engine in the strict sense of the term – it is a hierarchical index of Websites. As authors of Web pages have to submit sites to *Yahoo!* (the engine does not employ a spider or robot utility), *Yahoo!* will retrieve a smaller set of results than some other engines, but those results will generally be very tightly focused. It is possible to find appropriate sites quickly with only the smallest amount of information about the subject being researched, and the structure of the engine provides an excellent overview of a particular subject.

Other index-based search engines

The structure of *Yahoo!* is very appealing, both for organizations establishing Web search engines and also for those people who are new to searching. Consequently, it is an approach which is becoming more widely used. As we have already seen, traditional free-text search engines are now beginning to incorporate a directory structure, and it is becoming more difficult to classify search engines into different types. However, there are a number of other search engines which have their historical roots based firmly in the directory structure, and I'll point out some others which you may wish to look at, in much the same way that I did with free-text search engines.

Magellan

The *Magellan* home page at **http://www.mckinley.com** is shown in Figure 4.9.

As you can see, both *Magellan* and *Yahoo!* use the same basic approach of broad subject headings with narrower subheadings below, but while the basic structure is the same, *Magellan* has a number of different features. You can search using the hierarchical approach, but it is also possible to search the 60,000 sites which have been reviewed, although the reviews seem to be descriptive rather than analytical. An interesting feature are the "Green light sites"; these sites have been checked and those which have "adult" content have been screened out, ensuring that users will have no nasty surprises

DID YOU KNOW?
Adult material appears in the most surprising places. I once ran a search on my name, Phil Bradley, only to discover a large number of pornographic sites were listed. Upon investigation, it turned out that there is a gay porn star in the USA who shares the same name!

Fig. 4.9 *The "Magellan Internet Guide"*

when they click on links.

Magellan allows for "advanced searching," which allows you to make use of the usual '+', '-' and " " for phrase searching. However, you can also use Boolean operators AND, OR, AND NOT, as well as parentheses, for more complex searching.

Net Find, *G.O.D.* and *Excite*

Three other sites, all very similar in concept and approach, are *Net Find* at **http://www.net-find.com**, the *Global Online Directory* at **http://www.god.co.uk**, and *Excite* at **http://www.excite.com**. Since they are alike I have just listed the different major categories that they use below.

Net Find

Gamble	Business	Internet
Finance	Health	Electronics
Insurance	Home	Shopping
Computer	Real Estate	Marketing

G.O.D.

Arts and Crafts	Business
Community and Education	Entertainment
Financial Services	Games
Hot and Sexy	Internet Resources
Leisure and Pleasure	Paranormal
Personal Home Pages	Sports
Technology and Computers	Travel

Excite

Autos	Investing
Computers	Lifestyle
Entertainment	Music
Games	Relationships
Health	Sports
Home/Real Estate	Travel

This nicely illustrates that many of the index-based search engines are designed for rather more generalized and recreational uses, rather than academic or work-related use. None of them approaches the depth of coverage provided by *Yahoo!*, though this does not of course invalidate their use and value in certain situations.

Additional index-based search engines

Galaxy Tradewave: **http://galaxy.tradewave.com**
No Search: **http://www.nosearch.com**

Summary

Index-based search engines provide users with a straightforward approach to finding information by guiding them through a series of headings and subheadings until they are able to locate the information that they require. As a result they are very useful if you need to obtain an overview of a subject, or if you have a limited amount of knowledge about a subject. While all engines of this type provide headings, some are more in-depth than others, and your choice of engine should take this into account.

URLs mentioned in this chapter

http://www.yahoo.com
http://www.yahoo.co.uk
http://www.mckinley.com
http://www.net-find.com
http://www.god.co.uk
http://www.excite.com
http://galaxy.tradewave.com
http://www.nosearch.com

5

Multi-search engines

Introduction

We have now looked at a variety of different search engines, and it is worth emphasizing that they make up a very small percentage of the total number that are available. Each of them has its own strengths and weaknesses, and you will have discovered that you may need to use several of them to be confident that you have found everything that you need. This can be a time-consuming and frustrating experience, since you will often find references to exactly the same site from a number of different engines.

However, there is a solution to this problem, which is to make use of multi- or meta-search engines. This chapter concentrates on explaining what multi-search engines do and the different types. In common with the previous chapters, I take an in-depth look at one in particular.

What is a multi-search engine?

As the name implies, it is an engine that searches across multiple search engines on your behalf, displaying records on the screen in any one of a number of different formats. There are a variety of types of multi-search engine available, with their own strengths and weaknesses.

The simplest form is not really a multi-search engine at all, but simply a collection of links to different search engines, which may or may not include a dialog box to enable you to input search terms. Once the search has been input, you will be taken directly to the chosen search engine's home page to view the results.

The second type of multi-search engine allows you to input your search into a single dialog box, and in some cases to choose the search engines you want interrogated. The multi-search engine passes the query onto the chosen engines and displays the results, usually arranged in order of search engine.

The final type of multi-search engine is rather more sophisticated – it does all that the previous type does, but then de-duplicates the records to remove sites which are mentioned twice or more, and attempts to sort all the records into a more useful order.

As each of these multi-search engines takes a different approach, let's look at them a little more closely.

Before moving on to look at some examples of types of search engines, let's begin by taking a look at a few of their criteria in a little more detail.

Characteristics of multi-search engines

I have tried to put together a list of the different elements that one might expect to appear on a multi-search engine page. Unfortunately few, if any, of the multi-search engines exhibit all of these elements, and indeed some will have very few of them.

The number of search engines that a multi-search engine will use

The number of search engines that are used varies dramatically – the smallest in the sample that I looked at only referred to half a dozen, while the largest in the sample gave me access to over 1000 search engines, or database front ends. This is no real indicator of quality, however: it depends much more on the particular search engines that are used (and also their variety) rather than the sheer number. I would much prefer to use a multi-search engine that referenced a small number of what I would consider high quality search engines rather than a much larger number of engines that I did not really know or trust. Nonetheless, I think it is an acceptable criterion to use when evaluating the effectiveness of a multi-search engine; while more is not necessarily better, less could certainly be considered worse. While I would not normally evaluate success in terms of the number of hits, this is one of the reasons for using a multi-search engine, so it is probably justified.

The elements of the Internet that are searched

It seems almost automatic these days to regard the phrase "Search the Web" as a synonym for "Search the Internet." Of course, while that is understandable, given the hype and attention surrounding the World Wide Web, it behooves us to remember that there are a number of other aspects of the Internet which deserve consideration as well, such as usenet newsgroups, individual e-mail addresses and so on. Multi-search engines are at the mercy of the search engines they choose to reference, but given that there are a good number of these that concentrate on specific aspects such as those just mentioned, there is no reason why they should not be made available for searching as well.

Any words, all words, phrase searching

Again, there is little that the multi-search engine can do directly about this since it is unable to affect the internal workings of individual search engines. However, it is an option that should be offered to the end-user; if one search engine can search on a phrase out of the list available, it seems short-sighted not to offer this. Other engines on the list will simply ignore the phrase aspect and search on the words using an implied OR. If this is not given as an option, though, it reduces the effectiveness of those search engines that can undertake phrase searching. It seems to be an obvious point, but is one that was overlooked by some of the multi-search engines that I looked at.

Boolean operators, truncation and proximity searching

The very same comment can be made here as immediately above. A multi-search engine should provide and reflect the variety of approaches made available by the engines it references, but all too often this is not the case.

Focusing a search

There are of course many occasions when the user will not wish to do a global search, but will want to focus on one aspect specifically, such as searching in a specific domain (such as .com) or in a geographical area (such as Europe). Yet again, some search engines allow the user to focus the search this way, but this is not always reflected in the interface offered by the multi-search engine.

Choice of subject area

This approach is very familiar to anyone who has ever used the index approach to search engines, by taking a broad subject area and choosing various subheadings until the specific subject is reached. It is well known to all of us in the information profession that much of the time we don't want everything on a subject, but wish to focus on the medical or legal aspects, for example. Some multi-search engines do offer the facility to choose a specific subject focus, or indeed provide a subset of search engines that cover a particular subject area, and *The Big Hub* at **http://www. thebighub.com** and *CNET* at **http://www.search.com** deserve to be singled out here for being quite superb in this approach.

Time taken and hits returned

Here are two important elements, which both affect the amount of time that it takes to run some of these searches. A major disadvantage of using a multi-search engine is that you are very much left in the hands of the engines referenced. If they decide to take a long time to return a result, or they are particularly comprehensive, you may be left twiddling your thumbs while they work. By limiting the search either by number of hits or by getting the search to end after a particular period of time, you are able to exert at least a little control over the whole process. The danger here of course is that you are not going to achieve the same level of comprehensiveness that you might otherwise have, but at least you are being given the choice

Display

Many search engines will offer you a choice of three display modes: brief, normal or verbose. Your choice is likely to depend on what you actually want from the search, and the variety can be quite helpful in some circumstances.

Collating results

When you use a single search engine it is not uncommon to find the same site turning up as a hit several times – de-duping does not seem to be that much of a priority for a lot of developers! This problem is exacerbated when you do a multi-search; it can be annoying to retrieve what appears to be a reasonable number of hits, only to find that there are a great many duplicates in the list. In my opinion, one of the key strengths of a good multi-search engine should be that it is able to collate the results, de-dupe and then display. Unfortunately, however, there would appear to be very few multi-search engines that do this.

Help screens/FAQs

It is slightly distressing to see so many Internet retrieval engines attempt to give users the impression that searching is a very simple process, when of course we know it's rather more complex than that. All too often I log on to a multi-search engine page to find no instructions, no hints on how to create a better or more effective search, and no way of identifying how many search engines were used. Indeed, the lack of such information is quite astonishing. Perhaps it's just me, but if I'd taken a lot of time to create a multi-search interface, I'd want everyone to know who I was, how I had done it and why it was effective. It's possible that the producers of these facilities have rather smaller egos than I have, but I tend to attribute it rather more to laziness than anything else.

Types of multi-search engine

Having looked at some of the characteristics, we can now look at some of the different types, together with examples.

A straightforward list of different search engines

These multi-search engines work by simply copying the appropriate URL for the CGI script onto the Web page. This is not particularly difficult to do and you then simply input the appropriate search term(s) into the dialog box and submit the search. This is then run by the search engine in particular and you are presented with a list of results in exactly the same way that you would be if you had gone to visit that particular site directly. The advantage of this approach is simply that you can reduce the amount of time you spend going from one site to another in order to complete your search. It might also suggest other search engines that you had not considered using before. It is almost impossible to keep up with all of the different search engines that are available, and if someone is happy to do this on your behalf, it makes sense to take advantage of it.

However, the disadvantage of this approach is that, strictly speaking, these sites are (in my opinion) misleading the user. They are not offering a multi-search engine, but have simply collated the work of others on a new home page. That's not

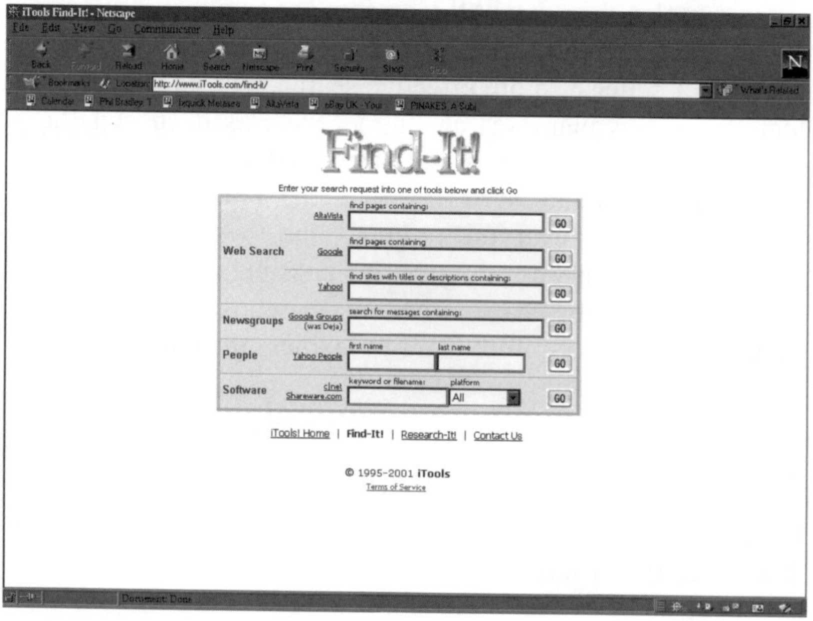

Fig. 5.1   *The "Find-It!" interface*
The copyright and trademark to "Find-It!" is held by "iTools.com"

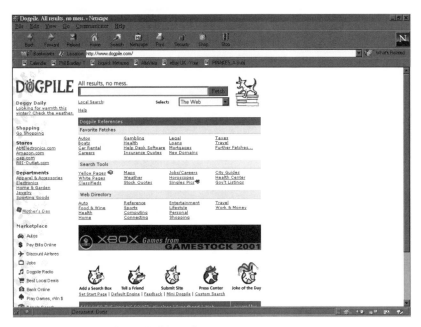

Fig. 5.2 *The "Dogpile" interface*

to say there is anything intrinsically wrong with this, and the Webmaster will have had to do a reasonable amount of work to set the page up, but it's really nothing more than a slightly more sophisticated list of links. This is by far the most common site offering a multi-search facility, and an example of a site that takes this approach is *Find-It!* at **http://www.iTools. com/find-it/** (you can see their interface in Figure 5.1).

Search results displayed once they are complete

This is much closer to the concept of a multi-search engine. A site of this nature will usually have a single-entry line where you input the search, just as you would with a single search engine interface. You may then have the opportunity of deciding which search engines you want the search to run under (usually from a list given in a check-box or similar) and the multi-search engine then transmits the search simultaneously to all of the search engines you have indicated.

Once the search has been run, the results will be displayed on screen as a list, commonly subdivided into the results as provided by the different search engines. However, the main

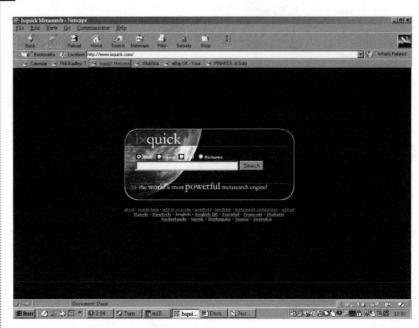

Fig. 5.3 *The "Ixquick"™ interface*

disadvantage of this type of approach is that, before the list can be generated on screen, all the different search engines have to send their results back to the multi-search engine site. Consequently, the speed of the search is dictated by the speed of the slowest search engine. An example of this type of search engine can be found on *Dogpile* at **http://www. dogpile.com/** (their interface is shown in Figure 5.2).

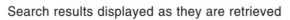

Search results displayed as they are retrieved

This type of search engine is very similar to the previous approach, the main difference being that searches do not have to wait until each search engine has completed its work – as soon as results are available from one search engine, they are displayed on screen for you to view. The result is that much faster, and while you are browsing down through the list of hits, others are being added to the page even as you view. An example of the multi-search engines which take this approach is *Ixquick*™ at **http://www.ixquick.com** (the interface is shown in Figure 5.3).

DID YOU KNOW?

Ever wondered what everyone is actually searching for? Visit http://www. metaspy.com to see the search terms people use. There is a filtered and an unfiltered link, which is updated every 15 seconds.

An in-depth look at *Ixquick*

As will have become clear from my previous comments, my preferred type of multi-search engine is the third type, and I find that of all those available, *Ixquick* is the one that most closely matches my needs. It uses a total of 12 different search engines, de-duplicates the results and displays them on the page using a relevance-ranked order based on the number of search engines which have found a particular page in their top ten lists of results, with a secondary ranking on the position of the page in the top ten.

This can easily be seen in Figure 5.4, which shows the result of a search done on my own name. You can see that my site comes right at the very top of the list, firstly because my home page has been highly ranked by a large number of search engines, and secondly because they find that page in high-ranking positions. One of the strengths, therefore, of *Ixquick* is that it works in conjunction with the ranking system used by a variety of search engines, rather than taking all the results and applying its own algorithms.

However, it is rather more sophisticated than simply doing

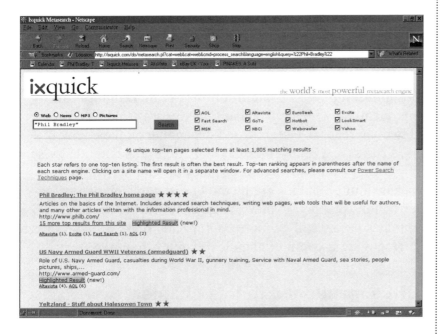

Fig. 5.4　　The results of a search on "Ixquick"™

that. As previously stated, a problem with many search engines in this category is that they will simply pass on the exact search string to individual search engines, regardless of whether or not the search engine will understand what is being asked. So, while one search engine may well realize that a search for *title:library* means that the searcher wishes to find the word "library" in the title element, another search engine may well assume that the search is for the particular string "title:library" and return no results! However, *Ixquick* is able to recognize the search that has been requested, and it will only pass that search on to those engines that understand the syntax and can deal with it accordingly. As a result, therefore, the level of relevance remains high. *Ixquick* knows which search engines can handle wildcards, multiple wildcards, wildcards in phrases, wildcards at the start of a word, and so on. These searches are translated by *Ixquick* and forwarded to the search engines that can properly deal with them.

Ixquick also has several other search features – not only does it search the Web, but by the use of the various radio buttons (which can be seen above the search box in Figure 5.3 and Figure 5.4) it is possible to search usenet newsgroups, MP3 files and pictures, using different sets of search engines as appropriate.

Summary

In summary, therefore, multi- or meta-search engines can provide users with a quick and effective way to do a reasonably comprehensive search, and depending on the engine used can save a lot of time and pick up results that otherwise might well be missed. However, they are not perfect by any means, limited as they are by the lowest common denominator factor, so although they can be excellent for quick searches it may still be more appropriate to use a single search engine if an in-depth or complex search is required.

URLs mentioned in this chapter

http://www.thebighub.com
http://www.search.com
http://www.metaspy.com

http://www.iTools.com/find-it/
http://www.dogpile.com/
http://www.ixquick.com

6

Natural-language search engines

Introduction

A recent development in the field of search engine technology is the introduction of what may be termed natural-language search engines – that is to say, a search engine which not only understands the request that has been made, but is able to interpret the question and come up with answers about the subject that are not entirely based on the words or phrases used by the questioner. For example, if you were interested in tax revenues in the UK, a natural-language search engine would understand that you were interested in business, finance and economics and would search accordingly.

As a result, search engines of this type are very useful if you really do not know what terms to look for, or if you have a very factual question that you need an answer to. If you're still trying to make sense of this, I can offer a personal example which may well help. I was recently asked for a list of gases that are partially soluble in water. Not having a chemistry background, I was a bit stuck to begin with. I didn't think that there would be much point in trying to use *AltaVista* or one of the other free-text search engines, since I wasn't sure of the best way to phrase my search. An index search engine wouldn't have been much help either, since I wouldn't have found a subsection under chemistry on "gases that are partially soluble in water." Since neither type of search engine would have been much use, there wasn't any point in going to a multi-search engine either, since I'd have exactly the same problem. However, I went to a natural-language search engine – *Ask Jeeves* at **http://www.aj.com** –

and posed the question 'Which gases are partially soluble in water?' The search engine came up with several results, all of which gave me the answers that I was looking for.

Ask Jeeves

As you can imagine, it's quite complicated to program a search engine to work in this manner, so there are very few of them available in this particular category. As I've already mentioned Ask Jeeves, though, let's start there. You can see the interface in Figure 6.1. Searches are written in a rather different way from that of free-text search engines, so if you wanted a list of good beaches in the USA you might run a search in AltaVista that looked something like: '+beach* + "United States,"* while in Ask Jeeves you could simply ask the question 'What are the best beaches in America?' The search engine is then able to take the query, overlay it with its own syntax in the background and provide you with a series of results.

Ask Jeeves provides a series of different answers to the questions asked, by providing access to different types of information. I asked the very simple question "Who won the Civil War?" and was given a series of answers as follows:

DID YOU KNOW?
Jeeves, from the Ask Jeeves search engine has been signed up by the Hollywood agent Michael Ovitz.

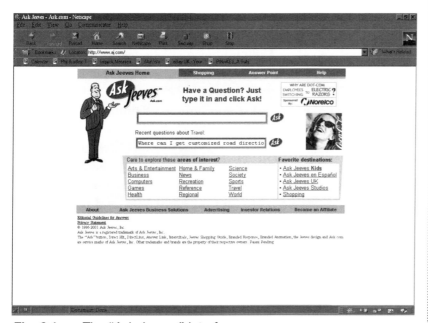

Fig. 6.1 *The "Ask Jeeves" interface*
© 1996–2001 Ask Jeeves Inc.

➤ Where can I learn about: The American Civil War (with a pull-down menu listing several other wars as well)

➤ Where can I find an introduction to the American history topic: The Civil War era (with a list of other eras available as pull-down menu options)

➤ Where can I learn about the American Civil War battle: (with a list of different battles in a pull-down menu)

➤ How can I subscribe to the magazine *America's Civil War* (with a listing of other magazines)

➤ Where can I find hints, codes and cheats for the PC game: (with a list of different games).

Below this list came another section entitled "People with similar questions have found these sites relevant:" with 10 Websites that were particularly appropriate to my question. Next I was provided with a section called "You may also wish to try these related searches:" which listed another 10 searches. Finally, I could choose to follow up my query by going to two other search engines that *Ask Jeeves* recommended to see what answers they could provide.

Ask Jeeves also has a secondary method of searching for information, akin to that used by *Yahoo!* If you take another look at Figure 6.1 you can see that there is an option "Care to explore these areas of interest?" and if you click on any of them you will be taken to a sub-menu and finally to a list of appropriate Websites. The number of Websites listed is, however, very small – in the region of 10–20 in most categories – so it really is no substitute for *Yahoo!* or another index search engine, but may be useful if you only have limited time available to run your search.

Ask Jeeves has a UK version at **http://www.ask.co.uk/** which works in exactly the same way, although the answers, unsurprisingly, tend to focus much more on the UK. I repeated my question regarding the Civil War, and the first few options I was given related to the English Civil War, although a secondary section listing results was culled from the American version of the search engine.

Other similar search engines

There are very few other natural-language search engines currently available: the only other one of note – *Albert* – is still in test mode, but it can be found at **http://www.albert. com/demo.php**.

Summary

In summary, a natural-language search engine can prove very useful if you're not exactly sure of what you want to find, you need to read around a subject area, or you're completely stuck! However, I have found that it's necessary to construct your question with as much care as with any other search engine: as well as the usual differences between American and UK words (such as football, for example), it's possible to mislead a natural-language search engine. If you asked for information about the Fred Astaire film *The Gay Divorcee* by just asking for information on that subject, you will obtain a lot of information about gay and lesbian matters, as well as advice on coping with divorce, and nothing on the film at all! However, to be fair, if you ask for information on the film, the results are much more appropriate.

URLs mentioned in this chapter

http://www.aj.com
http://www.ask.co.uk/
http://www.albert.com/demo.php

7

Finding images, sounds and multimedia information

Introduction

Images form an integral part of the Internet, appearing on just about every Web page that you look at. There are probably two reasons why you might be looking for images on the Internet – either to include them in a Web page that you're writing for yourself, in which case you'll be looking for icons, bullets, backgrounds and other assorted graphics, or in order to answer a query that you've been asked about. Sound files of one sort or another are available in abundance on the Internet – either as brief snippets of sound or as full-length songs. Multimedia is increasingly becoming a common format in which to provide information, although it still takes many hours to download a full-length movie, even with the fastest of connections! This chapter should hopefully provide you with some help in finding all types of media, for whatever purpose you require.

At this point, however, I should add a disclaimer: much of the material that you find (particularly sound files such as music files produced by pop groups) has been placed there without the agreement of the copyright holder. Copying this information may therefore be in breach of various Copyright acts, and unless you are certain that you are legally entitled to copy and use the file for the purpose you require, it makes sense to contact the copyright holder and seek specific permission.

Finding images on the Internet

Image formats

There are essentially two different types of image that you'll find on the Internet, and they'll have the extention .gif or .jpg. There are a small number of other file types that are slowly becoming more popular, but I'd be prepared to say that 99% of all the images you find will be in one or other of these formats. Photographs are generally to be found as .jpg images, while icon and cartoon type pictures with lots of block color will be found as .gif images. For the most part, you can ignore this, although it may be important if you want a specific type of image for use on a Web page as an icon. You'll probably find it helpful to focus your search on .gif images in that case. Alternatively, if you're looking for photographs, they will most likely be found as .jpg images. However, this is not a hard and fast rule, so while limiting yourself to a particular file type may give you a smaller number of hits, you may be excluding other images that would work perfectly well for whatever your purposes happen to be.

Using standard search engines to find images

Most of the standard search engines will provide you with some basic methods of searching for images, and the following are some examples of how you can quickly find images.

AltaVista

There are two methods of finding images at *AltaVista*. The first is to use the switch *image:* to locate any images that have a specific name. Consequently, if you are searching for images of the ship the Titanic, you could run a search like *image:titanic*, and that will return hits of Web pages that include any images called "titanic" on them. You could focus your search a little more closely by doing a search for *image:titanic.jpg* to try and retrieve mainly photographs. The problem here of course is that there is no saying that an image called "titanic" is going to be of the ship – it might be a still from the film, or indeed anything that the Web author thinks deserves the name "titanic." Consequently, you will probably want to use the *image:* switch in conjunction with some other search terms. In this example, I would probably try and narrow my search down to something more specific by doing a search on *AltaVista* such as: *image:titanic ship iceberg "maiden voyage"*, which should go a long way to excluding references to other types of "titanic."

The second way of searching for images at *AltaVista* is to use their picture finder. This is a specialized search engine which looks for images on Web pages, and should prove reasonably useful. At this point I would caution you to consider using the filtered version of this image finder – you might be amazed at the number of undesirable images that it is possible to unearth with even the most innocent of words! The interface is simple and straightforward to use, and you have the choice of looking for pictures or moving images, for example. Once *AltaVista* has returned the hits to you, it's simply a case of paging through them until you find the one that is suitable for your purposes. You may want to try the option of finding images that are similar, but in my personal experience this does not work terribly well, though you might always be lucky, of course!

HotBot

HotBot allows you to input the term that you're interested in and instead of searching for it in the text of Web pages, it will look for Web pages that contain images of that name. You can find this by choosing the advanced search function, and ticking the images box.

Lycos

By choosing the advanced search function, simply inputting the term that you are interested in to the search box, and clicking on the pictures option, you can limit your search to images rather than text on Web pages.

Yahoo!

In common with *AltaVista*, *Yahoo!* provides several ways of finding images. Perhaps the most straightforward way is simply to type the term "image" or "graphics" into the search box. Running a search for "images" lists 31 categories and 9045 individual sites, so it is probably best used to give yourself an overview of the images that are available in different subject areas such as "Government > U.S. Government > Military > Navy > Submarines > Images," for example. If you are particularly interested in obtaining graphics for Web pages, *Yahoo!* is probably the single best source to use. Simply search for "Web page images" and you'll get several hits to places in the *Yahoo!* hierarchy that will be of assistance.

Yahoo! also has an image search engine, but surprisingly, this is not apparent from their opening Web page. The *Image Surfer* can be found at **http://gallery.yahoo.com/** and currently has twelve different categories including: art, entertainment, history, science and travel. You can either search for a specific term, or you can simply browse through the list of categories, although this does rely very heavily on luck if you are to get good results.

Image-specific search engines

Stopstock at **http://www.1stopstock.com/** gives access to 12 different commercial image providers, and their databases can be accessed through the *Stopstock* front end. You can either do a multi-search across all providers, or if you prefer, search each individually. After the search has been run, you are presented with a list of images that match your search term, and these are kept deliberately in a low resolution. However, even having said that, the quality is quite acceptable for general viewing. The idea behind this is, of course, to encourage you to register with the image provider and purchase the particular image.

The *Amazing Picture Machine* at **http://www.ncrtec.org/picture.htm** is not what I'd call "amazing" myself, but it is simple, quick and easy to use. I suspect that their database is on the small size, since my search for "titanic" only came up with two images, but they were both on-topic. After the search has been run, you are provided with a summary of the results, and you can then choose to click on one in order to view the image. This is a nice touch, since it speeds up the whole process, and if your search yields a great many results, it's a quick and easy way of browsing through them without having to wait for all the images to load.

The *Sunsite ImageFinder* at **http://sunsite.berkeley.edu/ImageFinder/** is a collection of 10 individual image search engines which between them provide you with access to perhaps the biggest total collection of images on the Internet. There tends to be a bias towards America, such as images on Californian history, the American Memory and the Smithsonian, but it should be noted that there are also large collections of architectural images, 13,000 images from the Australian National Library and a link to the NASA images library server.

Webseek at **http://disney.ctr.columbia.edu/Webseek/** styles itself as a content-based image, video search and catalog tool. The format is the familiar *Yahoo!* approach, and the coverage is reasonably comprehensive, with 16 major categories to search in. My "titanic" search resulted in 239 hits, most of which were related to the ship. It was a fast and effective search engine and very easy to use.

Demon Image libraries and graphical counters

Demon Internet Services are one of the largest ISPs in the UK and they have put together a small list of image collections at **http://www.homepages.demon.co.uk/** that are designed to make it easier to add images to Web pages. Use is not restricted to Demon users, however, so if you want images on your pages, it might be worthwhile taking a look and following the links.

Aphids at **http://www.aphids.com/susan/imres/** is a personal collection of links to image libraries, as well as general information on images, image tools and references.

Image newsgroups

There are a great many newsgroups that are dedicated to images, though a depressingly large number of them are pornographic in content. People post photographs and images of different types and these can be saved using your newsreader and used for whatever purpose you want. Be warned, though, since a great many illegally copied images turn up in newsgroups, so you need to be extra careful before using them. The main hierarchy is alt.binaries.pictures.<something else>. Your newsreader can be used to track down the particular group that you're interested in, though be aware that if you are of faint heart you might be disturbed at some of the image newsgroups that you will see.

Finding sounds on the Internet

The good news is there are a lot of Web pages on the Internet that contain sound files, but the bad news is that the vast majority are of movie/tv clips and I suspect that they are in breach of copyright. Consequently, the warning that I gave at the beginning of the chapter applies especially to sound files – before you make use of sound files, please do check to make sure that you're allowed to use them. Some sites are explicit about what you can/cannot do with sound files, particularly those of film studios and record labels. Many of the sound libraries that you'll find have collected files from a variety of places, and they may not have been so rigorous in obtaining permissions to include the sounds that they make available. Therefore, if in doubt, check first!

Search engines

An increasing number of search engines will now give you the option of searching for sounds or Web pages that contain sounds. The *Altavista Media and Topic* search function at **http://search.altavista.com/sites/search/topic**, with options for products, directories, images, video and MP3/audio, allows you to search for Web pages that contain certain sounds or video clips, for example. A good practice search to try is "sean connery" and this should return pages that have sound files or video clips that are either of the actor Sean Connery or impressions of him.

Lycos and *HotBot* also have sound options that you can choose when doing a search – with *Lycos*, you can just click on the sound and pictures option, and with *HotBot* you can choose to include audio in the advanced options.

Websites

There are a lot of Websites that are simply libraries of sound files. Some of those that I use are:

➤ *The Daily Wav* at **http://www.dailywav.com/** (a .wav is a type of sound file, and this site has collected several thousand, although the majority of them are from film or television shows)

➤ *Moviesounds* at http://www.moviesounds.com/ (no prizes for guessing the subject content of this site!)

➤ *Sound America* at **http://www.soundamerica.com/** where the emphasis is on all things American, though once again there is a heavy preponderance of movie and television-related sounds.

If your interest is in popular music, probably the most infamous site to visit is *Napster* at **http://www.napster.com/**, which has been at the center of many legal disputes because of the way in which popular music tracks and albums can be downloaded from the Internet using their software. The site is (at the time of writing) still up and running, but there have been (and still are) continued threats to shut it down.

If you require more "professional" sounds (however you wish to define that) Gary Price (**http://gwis2.circ.gwu.edu/_gprice/speech.htm**) has compiled an impressive listing of speeches and transcripts covering US Presidential addresses, National Public Radio Programming Archives, keynote speeches from various business leaders, television and radio programs, US city and state officials, international governments/NGOs and think tanks, professional/trade associations, and historic material, for example. He has also produced an excellent page of links on current awareness resources via *Streaming Audio & Video*, which provides access to live (continuous feed) sites, news on the hour, international broadcasters, government, public radio (US), business news and events, special events, academia and additional directories.

An excellent article written by James Maguire on finding and using sounds on the Internet is at **http://mmsound. about.com/compute/mmsound/mbody.htm**.

Newsgroups

There are well over 100 newsgroups that people will post sounds to. You can be virtually certain that each and every one of these does not have copyright clearance! For more information on newsgroups, please see Chapter 12.

How do I play them?

Well, it depends entirely on the type of sound file, and on your having the appropriate plug-in utility available. The majority of files are going to be .wav or .mid files; you can simply click on the link for the file and your browser will then open a small window on the page and collect the file for you. You can then play it using the Windows default audio player. It should do this automatically, but you can replay it or save it if you wish to.

You may sometimes find that there are other types of sound file, such as MP3 files. To save going into great detail here, you should almost always find that, if a site makes use of files that you cannot automatically play, it will include a link to a site where you can download an appropriate plug-in utility. Go to the appropriate site, download and install the utility, and you'll then have no problem listening to the file.

Multimedia

So far we have looked at images and sound files, but of course there are other formats, such as moving images. These can be found using a variety of search engines; *AltaVista* has a specific search interface for video, as does *HotBot* (multimedia search) for example. There is a small number of search engines which have been specifically designed to find multimedia data, such as *Singingfish* at **http://www. Singingfish.com/**, which provides access to a wide variety of music, news, movies, sports, TV, radio, finance and live events. *Mediafind* at **http://search.digitide.de/** is another useful engine, providing access to a wide variety of different types of media.

Video files are available on the Internet in a variety of different formats, such as Quicktime, .mpg and Real Movie. In

DID YOU KNOW?
MP3audiobooks.com was bought for $8 million in February 2000, and currently holds the record for the most expensive purchase of a domain name.

order to view a video clip it will be necessary to have the appropriate software installed on your machine. Since different software packages are required for different formats there is little point in installing these until you require them – when this is necessary your browser will alert you to the need to install the software and wil guide you to a Website where it can be downloaded, and you should also be given this information on the Web page which contains a link to the video clip. However, if you do wish to explore the different packages available, a good resource is the *Tucows* site at **http://www.tucows.com/** – simply choose your operating system (such as Windows 98) and then find the option for multimedia tools, at which point you will be offered a wide selection of products. Please be aware that downloading multimedia files such as video clips can take a very long time, so prepare to be patient!

Summary

While there is still of course a preponderance of text on the Internet (and always will be), data is increasingly made available in a variety of other forms. It's always worthwhile considering the possibility that the information you require may be available as a sound file, picture or moving image. It is, however, more difficult to find information in formats other than text, if for no other reason than it's more difficult to index the information found in a multimedia format, so perhaps the best way of finding data is to look for a site that may possibly contain images or sound files first, and then search the actual site for the particular information that you require.

URLs mentioned in this chapter

http://gallery.yahoo.com/
http://www.1stopstock.com/
http://www.ncrtec.org/picture.htm
http://sunsite.berkeley.edu/ImageFinder/
http://disney.ctr.columbia.edu/Webseek/
http://www.homepages.demon.co.uk/
http://www.aphids.com/susan/imres/
http://search.altavista.com/sites/search/topic

http://www.dailywav.com/
http://www.moviesounds.com/
http://www.soundamerica.com/
http://www.napster.com/
http://gwis2.circ.gwu.edu/_gprice/speech.htm
http://mmsound.about.com/compute/mmsound/
    mbody.htm
http://www.Singingfish.com/
http://search.digitide.de/
http://www.tucows.com/

8

Finding people

Introduction

If you talk to people about the Internet, and specifically ask what they think it is, you will of course get a wide variety of answers: technical support people will tell you all about the computers and protocols used to link everything together; information professionals will wax lyrical about the information that can be found and used; sales people will tell you what a great tool it is for selling products, and so on. However, what many of them will not think of saying is that, when it comes down to it, the Internet is about people. It is people who make the computers, create the protocols; it is people who put up information, and it is, once again, people who will be buying products. So really what the Internet is about is people, plain and simple. As such, the Internet is a great way to find out all about them, often in much more detail than you would expect. This chapter deals with some of the ways that you can locate particular people, and find out more about them.

There are basically four different ways of looking for people on the Internet: you can use the standard search engines to just look for references to someone's name, and then visit the Website(s) that are returned to you; you can use search engines that look for a name and relate that to an e-mail address; you can use a "people finder" to look for particular individuals; or finally you can use a small number of very specific resources. In this chapter I'll cover all these methods, and try to assess (in a very non-scientific way) how useful each of these proved to be when I attempted to use it.

Standard search engines

First of all, I tried doing some searches for "Phil Bradley" using *AltaVista* at **http://www.altavista.com**, *HotBot* at **http://www.hotbot.com**, *Lycos* at **http://www.lycos. co.uk**, and *Northern Light* at **http://www.northernlight. com** just to see what turned up. The results were as follows (the first number indicates the number of Web pages returned; the second number in brackets relates to the first time that "my" "Phil Bradley" turned up):

AltaVista	1,583	(1–3)
HotBot	560	(1)
Lycos	1,484	(1–10)
Northern Light	1,409	(8–10)

This was a pretty reasonable result, I felt. All four engines worked well, and since I write my Web pages so that search engines rank my name highly, it wasn't surprising that I got so many high-ranking results. Of course, if you don't know me in any detail, it will mean that you'll have to spend some time visiting the returned Web pages before you can find me, which shouldn't be that difficult since I'm neither a baseball player, nor a gay porn star! Consequently, using a general search engine to find a particular individual does have merit, provided you are fairly clear on exactly who you are looking for (a search that would have really focused closely on me as an individual would have added in some other search parameters such as "librarianship," for example). However, it won't necessarily provide you with much by the way of contact details, unless that information is included on a Web page, and this approach isn't going to work terribly well if the person you are looking for has a common name; there are over 130,000 references in AltaVista to "John Smith" for example!

E-mail search engines

There are a number of search engines which, as the name

DID YOU KNOW?
Americans receive 200 e-mails a day on average. Their British counterparts receive 171 on average.

implies, are simply databases of names matched to e-mail addresses. They collect their data from a variety of sources – from usenet newsgroup postings, from Web pages and from people who register directly with them.

Some of these are independent engines, while others are associated with the more general search engines. For example, *Yahoo!* has an e-mail search function at **http://people. yahoo.com/** and searching for my name returned over 60 different matches with "mine" being 16th in the list, although you would only really know that if you already knew my e-mail address, which rather invalidates the whole point of using the service! I also tried the *Excite* people finder, which returned over 400 matches, but because the service is limited to the USA I didn't bother to see if "my" name was listed.

Next I tried *I-Ring* at **http://www.i-ring.com/find/ find.cgi** which listed my e-mail address in ninth position, despite the fact that it appeared to be searching a predominately US database. However, once again it was only helpful because I already knew what my e-mail address was – the system doesn't provide any more information than a name and e-mail address you can mail to. Interestingly, *I-Ring* uses a multi-search approach, using information provided by four other services: *Bigfoot* at **http://www.bigfoot.com/**, *Infoseek* at **http://www.infospace.com/_1_4PW9TN503NB3D9I _info/redirs_all.htm?pgtarg=pplea**, *Whowhere* at **http:// www.whowhere.lycos.com/** and *Yahoo!*. But when I visited the *Infoseek* service I was able to get a little bit more information directly (including my geographical location in London). *The Internet @ddress Finder* at **http://www.iaf.net/ noframes-default.htm** only returned four results, mine being the second on the list, and it did not give any further information; it worked, though it could scarcely be called comprehensive.

People finders

These are rather more common than e-mail search engines, and they attempt to provide users with rather more information than just an e-mail address. When possible they will also give you telephone numbers, street addresses and, in the case of US residents, even maps of how to get to someone's home

– all rather spooky. They are usually connected to other services, allowing you to send virtual cards, or even gifts, to the people you find.

Once again, the big-name search engines come back into the picture here. *AltaVista* has a people finder at **http://worldpages.altavista.com/whitepages/**, and the emphasis is on the USA; you can either do a global search or limit the search to a US city or state. The global search that I ran gave me a total of 151 hits, but they were all versions of Phil Bradley (Phil, Philip, Phillip, Phillippa) in the US or Canada, so no luck there – though obviously it would be much more useful if you were looking for people based in either of those two countries.

Lycos uses the *Who Where? Database* at **http://www.whowhere.lycos.com/Phone** and it found over 100 references to Phil Bradley, but unlike most of the other engines, it also gave me a chance to search public records, find old high school friends, or call up a map of the address of any people listed in the results. Unfortunately *Lycos UK* doesn't provide the same functionality. (However, there are other options for locating people in the UK as discussed below.)

Excite also has a people finder at **http://wp.superpages.com/people.phtml?SRC=excite**, which is also US-based, and provides information on the person, their address and telephone number, a map, the option of finding neighbors and a link to driving instructions on how to get to their home! Once again, however, there wasn't an option to do the same sort of search on the UK version of the search engine.

While these major search engines do fall down when it comes to locating people based in the UK, there are a number of resources that can be used instead. An obvious example to begin with is the British Telecom directory search service at **http://www.bt.com/directory-enquiries/dq_home.jsp**. The interface can be seen in Figure 8.1. In order to use the service effectively, you already need to have a reasonable amount of information on the person that you're looking for. A search for Phil Bradley in London doesn't produce any results, but if the search is refined to include the area in London in which I live, my name, address and telephone number are returned. The service isn't comprehensive, since it doesn't include ex-directory numbers, but if

HINTS AND TIPS
Remember that some people use shortened versions of
their names or nicknames, so run searches which match
Phil and Philip, for example, whenever the search engine gives you that opportunity.

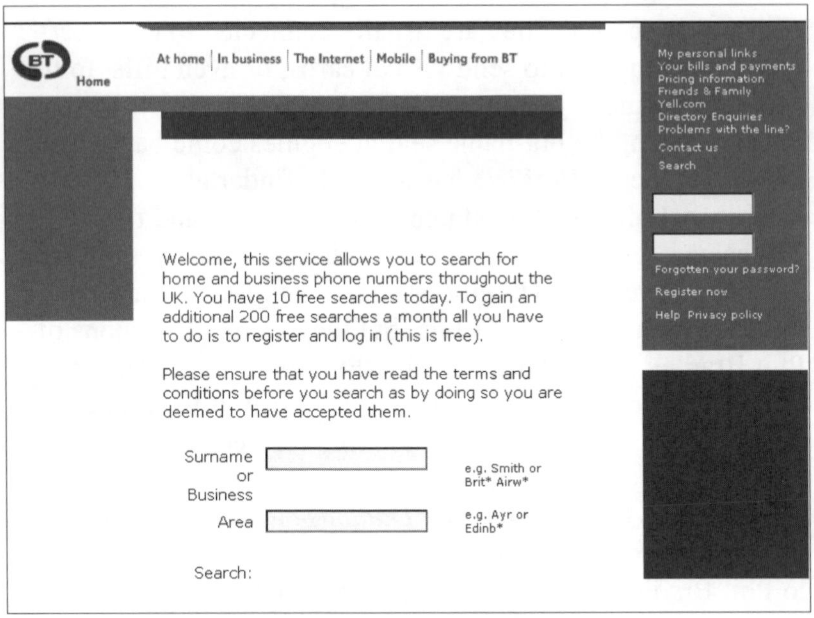

Fig. 8.1 *Part of the interface of the BT directory search service*
© *Courtesy of British Telecommunications plc*

you have a fair amount of information on the person you want to find, it's a useful resource.

192.com at **http://www.192.com** attempts to give a comprehensive coverage of people based in the UK by using information from a variety of different sources, both from the Internet and from other listings. Before using the service it is necessary to register (registration allows users to run a limited number of searches each month), but once you have registered a large number of resources are available, although for full access to the data a subscription is charged. *192.com* offers a people-search facility, the electoral roll, a family and relationship service, as well as a business-finding service, including company and director reports. *192.com* also provides a maps and addresses function, and the opportunity to search internationally, not just within the UK.

The people finder provided by *Infospace* at **http://www. infospaceuk.com** allows you to search on a name and location, and will attempt to provide a complete address and phone number. It also provides an international service for the USA, Canada and a number of major European countries as well.

Specific tracking services

There are a number of these available if you're trying to trace an old friend or a relative, for example.

LookupUK at **http://www.lookupUK.com** provides links to UK telephone services, e-mail search services for the UK and Ireland, and genealogical searches, and it also has a message board that allows you to post a message for the people that you're looking for, which is also searchable. It's probably a long shot to try and locate someone this way, but if all else fails it may be worth trying. Having said that, they do boast of considerable successes, so cross your fingers and post!

Friends Re-united is a Website that gives people the opportunity to link themselves to a specific school, and to see and then contact other people who were at that school at specific times. It's very comprehensive, very easy to use and a well-constructed site. It's certainly worth visiting at **http://www. friendsreunited.co.uk** in order to list yourself and check to see if you know anyone else who has also registered. The American equivalent is *Classmates* at **http://www. classmates.com/**, which has a list of 40,000 schools and 19,000,000 people listed.

Both of these databases are quite parochial, but if you're not from the UK, or want to find people from other countries, a good resource to use is the *Familysearch* database at **http://www.familysearch.org**, which is run by the Mormons. This has an excellent selection of genealogical resources online, allowing you to discover a lot of information about relatives, friends and ancestors.

It is also worth thinking laterally when it comes to looking for people. For example, if it is necessary to track down an academic, it may be worth looking at *Jiscmail* at **http://www. jiscmail.ac.uk/** (formerly known as *Mailbase*), which is the national academic mailing list service and is designed to facilitate discussion, collaboration and communication within the UK academic community and beyond. Although at the time of writing (May 2001) it does not have search facilities, these are planned for the near future, thus allowing people to search for individuals in the academic community, both in the UK and abroad.

A final useful resource for locating e-mail addresses is to

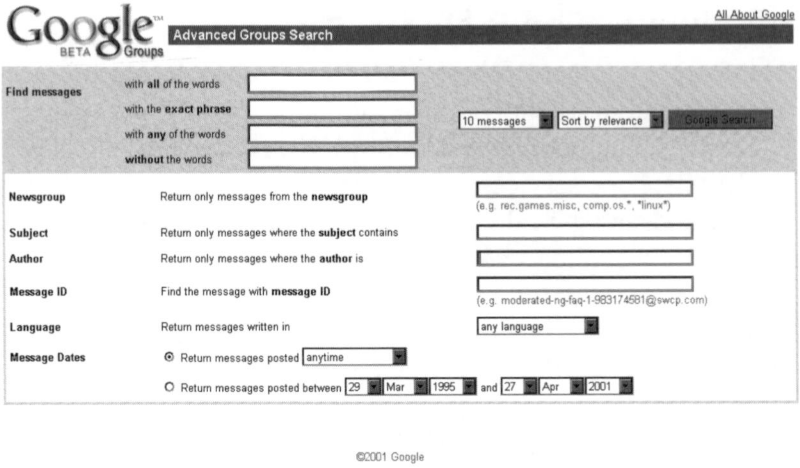

©2001 Google

Fig. 8.2 *"Google Groups" advanced search function*
Google Brand Features are trademarks of Google, Inc.

check to see if the individual you are interested in posts to usenet newsgroups (this is covered in more detail in Chapter 12). The source that used to be best for this was a service called *Deja* (previously *DejaNews*), which was recently taken over by *Google Groups*. It has an advanced search function, as shown in Figure 8.2, and if you simply type in the name of the person you are interested in locating into the author search box, you may strike lucky, though in all probability, unless the person has a very unusual name, you may need to spend time looking at a lot of posts before identifying the individual in question.

Summary

As with most Internet-related issues, there isn't generally one "best" way of searching for people, and as usual it may be necessary to match your particular requirements to the appropriate search engine for the job. However, with a little perseverance and time it may well often be possible to locate the particular individual that you want to track down, but the more information you have, the quicker the job will be.

URLs mentioned in this chapter

http://www.altavista.com
http://www.hotbot.com

http://www.lycos.co.uk
http://www.northernlight.com
http://people.yahoo.com/
http://www.i-ring.com/find/find.cgi
http://www.bigfoot.com/
http://www.infospace.com/_1_4PW9TN503NB3D9I
    _info/redirs_all.htm?pgtarg=pplea
http://www.whowhere.lycos.com/
http://www.iaf.net/noframes-default.htm
http://worldpages.altavista.com/whitepages/
http://www.whowhere.lycos.com/Phone
http://wp.superpages.com/people.phtml?SRC=excite
http://www.bt.com/directory-enquiries/dq_home.jsp.
http://www.192.com
http://www.infospaceuk.com
http://www.lookupUK.com
http://www.friendsreunited.co.uk
http://www.classmates.com/
http://www.familysearch.org
http://www.jiscmail.ac.uk/

9

Other available database resources

Introduction

Given the size of the Internet and the size of this book, it is not going to be possible to list every information resource that is available to the advanced searcher, or even to go into detail about what is available. However, I think it is important to try to point you towards as many different ways of obtaining information as I can, so this chapter brings together some of the other ways that you can find out information from Internet database resources.

Some of these are free resources, while others are ones that you have to subscribe to or pay for on a "pay as you go" basis. It is important that we cover these, since it is all too easy to limit yourself to using material which has been made available free. The advanced Internet searcher will, however, be aware of a wide variety of Internet resources, and should at least consider the possibility of using commercial as well as free ones.

Some of the resources that I look at in this chapter are:

➤ information provided free of charge by publishers
➤ online communities
➤ commercial information
➤ online journals
➤ newspapers
➤ bookshops
➤ paid services offered by search engines.

Freely available information provided by publishers

It sounds a little bit too good to be true, doesn't it? However, most publishers are indeed offering free material on the Internet that you might well expect to have to pay for. You may rest assured that they have sound financial reasons for providing this information as a "loss leader" – they hope that you will value the data enough to subscribe to the fully paid-up subscription-based service that they offer.

I'm aware that at this point I'm racing ahead a little bit, because I've started to talk about "publishers" without fully explaining what I mean. This is because the term "publisher" is becoming increasingly difficult to define clearly and neatly. In the "old days," if I can refer to a situation which existed 20 years ago as "old," a publisher was an organization which produced printed books or journals and then sold the result to you and me. With the arrival of online, this definition was expanded to include organizations (sometimes the same ones, but more often different organizations) which published in a digital format, first via large databases stored on mainframe computers, and then on optical discs, such as CD-ROM. The arrival of the Internet has made the definition much more difficult, since in a sense I "publish" articles that I write directly onto my Website, making me both author and publisher. Anyone who produces a Website and makes information available from it can, with a certain amount of justification, be described as a publisher. However, for clarity I am using "publisher" to refer to organizations which have previously made data available either in hard-copy form, or via an online database or in CD-ROM format.

These organizations are very keen to use the Internet, since it provides them with another means of making their data available, and so information professionals now have greater flexibility in deciding how to receive their data. I will return to this subject in Chapter 13, the information mix. All we need consider at the moment is the fact that one of the ways in which publishers are attracting customers is by offering data for nothing.

Each publisher provides different types of free information, and my first example is Kluwer Academic Publishers, at

http://www.wkap.nl/. You can obtain a full listing of their titles, details about each, and sample copies of journals; you can also view their tables of contents and some articles.

Sweet and Maxwell, a legal publisher with a Website at **http://www.smlawpub.co.uk/**, offers a whole raft of free information, such as current law case of the week, European current law case of the week, free online updates to administrative law, a court alerting service, and so on.

My next example of the work being done by electronic publishers comes from Chadwyck-Healey at **http://www. chadwyck.co.uk**. In common with other electronic publishers, they are making their products available across the Internet, accessed via a subscription and password. Once you have purchased a subscription, you can search and retrieve data from any of the subscribed databases.

Creating an online community

Some companies create an online community based around an area of shared interest. An example of this can be seen at BioMedNet's site at **http://www.bmn.com**. This is described as an "online club for the biological and medical research community" and already has over 876,000 members. Given that the figure given in the first edition of this title was 50,000 members, you can see how popular the service is! Membership is free upon registration, and this allows access to a library of full-text journals, biological databases, the MEDLINE database, a job exchange, discussion groups, a shopping mall and a members' magazine. Members can s earch all the databases, but viewing the full text of articles from partner publishers usually requires a payment or subscription to the product.

Organizations subscribing to BioMedNet can place funds into a central account, or can allocate funds to individuals, who can then fulfil their own information requirements. Individuals can also deposit funds into their own account by check or credit card.

As a result, users of the system are able to meet online and have discussions; they are informed about new developments in their areas of interest, notified about new publications, can search existing resources, download articles and generally

HINTS AND TIPS

If you are going to give an organization your credit-card details, make sure that they offer you a secure method of encrypting your details for transfer across the Internet. They should mention this on any Web page where you are asked for personal details. If in doubt, e-mail them to confirm that they do encrypt the details before you send them.

keep in daily contact with professionals and peers. This has proved to be so popular that other online clubs are quickly being established. Another example is ChemWeb, the world-wide club for the chemical community, which can be found at **http://chemWeb.com**.

Do keep in mind the existence of this material provided freely by publishers, since it will be of high quality, current and with a high level of authority. A disadvantage is that you cannot guarantee what information you will find, and it can be a little like going to a garage sale, but if you can identify those publishers who produce material that is relevant to your work, you can obtain some very useful information from them.

Commercial information

Commercial uses of the Internet could easily take up an entire book in their own right, and I do not intend to go into great detail here; most of what I want to say about commerce and the advanced searcher is covered in Chapter 13. However, it is worth pointing out that publishers are using the Internet to increase revenue, and if you have the budget, you can make use of these services. To illustrate this, I have two examples of companies that are doing a lot of work in this area, and you will be able to see how you can use their systems to obtain information to assist you in your daily work.

My first example is SilverPlatter Information, at **http://www.silverplatter.com**, one of the world's largest CD-ROM publishers, with a total of over 200 bibliographic and full-text electronic databases. SilverPlatter also provides access to over one million articles from premier electronic journals via their SilverLinker service (this is described further below). In common with many other publishers, they have now repositioned themselves in the market, and they would probably take exception to my description of them as "CD-ROM publishers," preferring to see themselves as "electronic publishers." Most electronic publishers are now ensuring that their customers have greater flexibility in accessing their data; they provide it on optical discs, but the databases can also be copied onto hard disk for faster access, and as a result of this there is no reason why data in this format can-

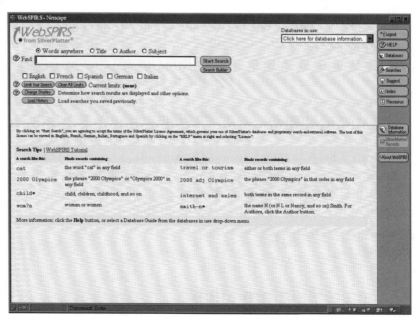

Fig. 9.1 *SilverPlatter's "WebSPIRS" interface*
WebSPIRS Version 4.01 Copyright 1995–1998 SilverPlatter
International NV

not be made available to subscribers across the Internet.
SilverPlatter has made a version of its search software called
WebSPIRS available on the Internet, and I have included a
screenshot as Figure 9.1

The interface provides access to all the functionality
SilverPlatter customers have come to expect: searching for a
word or phrase in the text, title, author and subject searches,
access to the database index or thesaurus (if available), and
searching by publication year. The reason for this is quite
clear – if end-users are familiar with the locally networked or
standalone product, they will be more likely to search the
database across the Internet if the interface looks familiar to
them, resulting in a much shallower learning curve. You can
run a search, and will be given a results screen similar to that
shown in Figure 9.2.

It is at this point that the power of using the Internet as a
delivery mechanism for information really comes into its
own. Certain elements of the displayed record (such as
author or journal, for example) can be highlighted, and those
users who are used to Internet conventions will realize that
they can click on the highlighted text in order to see all of the

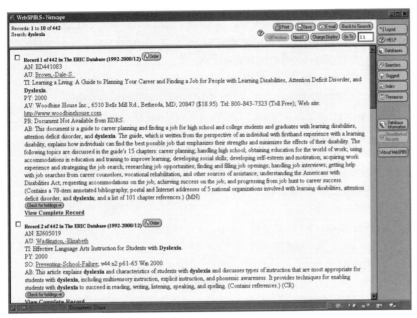

Fig. 9.2 *Partial results from searching a "WebSPIRS" database*
WebSPIRS Version 4.01 Copyright 1995–1998 SilverPlatter
International NV

articles in the database written by that author, or they can run a search to locate all the articles published in a particular journal. They can of course do the same thing using the traditional version of the software, but the hypertext linking makes the whole process that much more intuitive and straightforward.

The records can then be marked and printed, downloaded or sent via e-mail to a colleague; again the Internet is providing greater flexibility. However, there is more to a Web-based version than this simple level of flexibility, since by the very nature of the medium it becomes much easier to manipulate the data. SilverPlatter's SilverLinker service integrates the full text of journals and bibliographical databases, allowing direct access from the databases to electronic journals available on the Internet. Once an article has been located in a bibliographical search, you may be able to retrieve more information on it by interrogating the library holdings, or order it directly from your preferred document delivery supplier.

The consequences of this approach are clear: it is becoming much easier to dynamically integrate a variety of different systems to link data together for ease of searching and immediate delivery of that data. In the future, the end-user will be able to search for and locate appropriate articles, order the full text of an article and retrieve it via e-mail within a matter of moments, instead of days or weeks. Moreover, the user will be able to do this directly from his/her own desktop, without intervention from the information professional.

It is worth pointing out that *WebSPIRS* is available for you to try out free of charge. Although the available sample data-bases are quite small, all of the information is correct, so it may be worthwhile making use of them now and then for a brief overview of a particular subject, or to obtain a few quick references.

Similar work is being done by other electronic publishers, such as Ovid Technologies, based at **http://www.ovid.com**. Ovid aggregates content from its information providers via a single password and server, ensuring that users obtain seamless access to the data they require.

Once again, the implications of this are far-reaching. In the past, because of the nature of the medium, publishers presented data in the form of bound journals. Publishing a single small article of, say, four pages is not feasible for cost and distribu-tion reasons, but becomes possible when it is included with other articles in a journal. When publishing on the Internet, however, it becomes not only possible, but highly desirable, to make information available in discrete units that can be located and downloaded quickly and easily. As a result, questions can be asked about the future viability of journals in the form that we have known them for the last few hundred years.

The future role of printed journals also becomes less certain when we look at the question of currency. The result of taking an article, printing it and distributing it, is that currency is sacrificed on the altar of distribution. Electronic publication results in articles being published in a matter of minutes instead of weeks or months. Databases can be updated on a daily or hourly basis, instead of taking a month or longer to distribute in optical or paper format. Once again, this raises a number of questions for the long-term archiving and retrieval of information, which I will address in Chapter 13.

Online journals

I have already mentioned online journals in connection with

databases which can be accessed via the Internet, but it is important to make a distinction between those and journals which have their own separate "life" as electronic journals. There are literally thousands of electronic journals which offer high-quality information totally free of charge. These are often in receipt of funding from one organization or another, and exist to promote the free flow of information in their chosen subject area. Two good examples here are *American Libraries Online* (the Web version is at **http://www.ala.org**), which "provides news items of interest to librarians and information professionals" and the *Internet Resources Newsletter* at **http://www.hw.ac.uk/libWWW/irn/irn.html** (please note the capitalization in this URL), which is described as being "for academics, students, engineers, scientists and social scientists." Both journals are full of very useful information, and I make sure that I read every single issue (as well as contributing a search engine column to *Ariadne*). Both are available free of charge, and are very much in the tradition of making information freely available across the Internet.

In many cases, when electronic journals are first established, access to them is free. There are many reasons for this. First, potential readers need to be encouraged to visit the site, and since the publisher cannot give away a binder or free gift as with printed journals, free access can be regarded as a loss leader. Secondly, it is quite difficult to price access to an electronic journal in comparison with a printed version; should it be less, since the publisher does not have the printing and distribution overheads; the same price, since the quality of data should be the same; or indeed should it cost more, since readers are getting quicker access to information which can be presented in a wider variety of media? What is swiftly becoming clear to many publishers is that some sort of charge is necessary, since they have to pay writers, designers and programmers, and cover the equipment costs. Some of this money can be recouped by selling advertising space, but it is possible to find only so many advertisers!

Newspapers

Online newspapers, which for the sake of this chapter will be treated like other online journals (although there are significant differences), are another splendid source of information for searchers. When I ran a search on *Yahoo!* for newspapers I came up with 521 categories and 4900 sites, and I am sure this number will have increased by the time you get to read this. The range of newspapers is quite phenomenal, from regional or city titles such as the *San Francisco Chronicle* at **http://www.sfgate.com** to national newspapers such as the *Electronic Telegraph* at **http://www.telegraph.co.uk**.

Once again, each title is unique and arranges its material as it feels appropriate. Some titles are virtually identical to the paper edition, while others are entirely electronic, and yet others are a combination of these approaches. Some are updated several times during the day, others daily and others again weekly.

However they are updated, and whatever the precise content, online newspapers are one of the very best ways to keep up to date with what is happening within a specific region, city or country, or throughout the world. A sensible searcher will bookmark at least one or two newspapers to refer to regularly.

Bookshops

It is an obvious statement, but bookshops are a wonderful source of information. They do have a number of drawbacks, however, chiefly as a result of being a physical entity! It takes time to go and visit, you need to have a clear idea of what you are looking for, and you need to find the right set of shelves to start hunting through to find appropriate titles. Even when you finally alight on a likely title, you are still not sure it is going to be exactly what you want, so it is then necessary to spend time examining the book before purchasing it. Great fun, of course, but it does use up a frightening amount of time!

Internet bookshops overcome all of these disadvantages, and as a result have become very popular; *Yahoo!* lists a total of 5520 Web pages for Internet bookshops, including 151 based in the UK or Ireland. I'll just explore one in detail to illustrate their value to the information professional.

Amazon.com is one of the largest bookshops (if not the

largest) on the Internet, with over 2.5 million titles available, and over 15 million people from 160 countries have purchased titles from their site at **http://www.amazon.com** (or **http://www.amazon.co.uk** for the UK version). Amazon has taken an approach similar to that of BioMedNet, in that they have tried to create a community approach with their data. As well as a straightforward listing of their titles (which of course they have), they have a book-of-the-day section, with an overview of a title and the opportunity to read excerpts, reviews and interviews with the author. Their database can be searched in a number of different ways, by keyword, subject, author, ISBN, publisher, date of publication, and so on. As well as books, Amazon has expanded to sell popular music, videos, electronic goods, kitchen goods and so on. However, since I can't easily imagine a valid professional reason for running a search for pots and pans, I'll concentrate on looking at their more traditional offering of books.

I ran a search for "intelligent agents" and was presented with a list of their top three titles and 107 other matches. For most of those I was then able to view the table of contents, obtain a synopsis of the title, read information on the author, and read reviews from people who had already purchased the title. I was also presented with the opportunity to search for titles in related subject areas (one of which was electronic data processing, for example), and Amazon also provides a list of other titles purchased by people who had bought the title I was interested in. Another feature of the site is an automated searcher which informs you when any new titles are published that match criteria that you can set.

Needless to say, you can purchase any of the titles you are interested in (along with a variety of other merchandise such as CDs or T-shirts) by placing them in a "shopping cart" which keeps a running total of your expenditure. Once you are satisfied with your selection, your credit card is debited and the titles shipped, usually within a couple of days.

An Internet bookshop such as Amazon offers a useful and easy way to purchase titles, and given the discounts they make available, it is almost certainly cheaper to shop at Amazon even once post and packing charges are included than it is to visit your own local bookshop. It is also an excel-

DID YOU KNOW?

Entire books are available online which can be read using your browser or downloaded and printed out. This is not only the case for out-of-copyright publications, but also for some books which are still in copyright. A good example is Digital business, which is available at **http://www.hammond. co.uk** together with a detailed explanation from the author as to why he has made his title available in this way.

lent way to search for details of books in print. The reviews and guides to similar titles are also an extremely effective method of book selection, and could easily be used by an information professional who had been asked to create a bibliography for an inquirer.

Commercial search engines

As we have seen, most search engines are free for people to use; the organizations that provide them are currently making their money from selling advertising space. Their software is becoming increasingly sophisticated; if you run a search on *AltaVista* for information on gardens and flowers, you will probably find that you are viewing an advertisement for an Internet florist, for example. While it appears unlikely that the large search engines will charge for standard searches, they may well charge for some of the other services they provide. A good example here is the *Northern Light* search engine, based at **http://www.northernlight.com/**.
Northern Light is a free-text search engine, and people who have searched using *AltaVista* or *Lycos* will not find it difficult to use. The difference is that *Northern Light* provides access to what it calls its "special collection sources," which are not available anywhere else on the Internet. Most of these sources go back to January 1995, and some book reviews go back as far as 1990. The collection comprises over 7000 journals, books, reviews, magazines and newswires.

When searching *Northern Light*, you have the choice of searching the Web, the special collection or both for no charge. You are able to see abstracts from the special collection for free, but if you wish to view the entire article or document it is necessary to pay a fee. The organization justifies this by explaining that information from the special collection is high-quality, authoritative information which is worth paying for.

Payment is made online via a secure credit-card transaction (prices vary in general from $1.00 to $4.00), and the document is then displayed on your screen just as though it was another Web page. *Northern Light* does not offer a subscription service – the system is set up as a "pay as you go" service.

Summary

Effective searchers will not limit themselves to the major search engines or databases, but instead will keep a very open mind about using resources which come from many different sources. In this chapter we have looked at a variety of these, and discussed the ways in which they could be useful. The best information is not always free, and sometimes it is necessary to pay premium prices for premium data, but it is almost always possible to get some worthwhile information out of the free material provided by commercial organizations.

URLs mentioned in this chapter

http://www.wkap.nl/
http://www.smlawpub.co.uk/
http://www.chadwyck.co.uk
http://www.bmn.com
http://chemWeb.com.
http://www.silverplatter.com
http://www.forrester.com
http://www.ovid.com
http://www.ala.org
http://www.hw.ac.uk/libWWW/irn/irn.html
http://www.sfgate.com
http://www.telegraph.co.uk
http://www.amazon.com
http://www.amazon.co.uk
http://www.hammond.co.uk
http://www.northernlight.com/

10

Virtual libraries and gateways

Introduction

I have concentrated so far mainly on how to find information
on the Internet by using a variety of different search engines.
This is, of course, an effective way of obtaining information,
but it is not the only way. When, as a user, you go into a
library, you do not expect to have to start searching for information immediately; instead you make use of the signposting
available, or perhaps a map in order to get to the section you
are interested in. Moreover, when you get to the shelves you
expect that the books and other resources will have been
selected by the librarians to cover the subject area and to be
trustworthy sources of information.

This does not automatically happen on the Internet, unfortunately, since there is no librarian figure who can check the
authority of the data or provide you with all the appropriate
links. However, there do exist virtual libraries and gateways
that can assist in this area. In this chapter I begin by looking
at some of the ways in which you can assess and evaluate the
resources that you discover. Then I go on to consider the
steps that have been taken to provide users with signposts to
valuable information.

Authority on the Internet

This important statement is worth repeating: you cannot automatically trust the information that you find on the Web.
Since no one is in charge of it, anyone is free to make available almost any type of information that they wish. I say

"almost," since Web authors are constrained by the laws of the land. It is not legal for me to libel someone, and making a libellous statement on a Website will also leave me open to prosecution. However, apart from obvious areas such as that, I am free to write and publish anything I please, and there is no onus on me to ensure that it is factually accurate.

It is necessary, therefore, always to question the information that you find on the Web, and fortunately there are a few helpful ways of checking the authority of a Website.

The domain name

The first thing that I always check when looking at a Website is the URL. This tells you a lot about the level of trust you can put in the documents that you find.

You can be assured that if a Website has **.edu** in the URL it is definitely some sort of academic site, or if it includes **.gov** it is a government site. (The situation is different with respect to newsgroups or mailing lists, since even if **.edu** or **.gov** is included in an e-mail address, the individual may well be writing in a personal capacity.) You are slightly less secure with a commercial domain name ending in **.com**, as it is much easier to obtain these. Further, the **.com** domain name, once used almost exclusively by American commercial organizations, is now widely available, and indeed my own Website is at **www.philb.com** and I am neither American nor based in the USA; in fact the server which hosts my site is based in Manchester, England. Many Internet service providers are now offering free Web space, which is wonderful for budding authors, but simply adds to the confusion for searchers, as the domain name is usually a variant of the ISPs.

In the past it was very easy in many countries to register a domain name, and there were very few checks on who registered what. This has actually led to court cases brought by high-profile organizations that were not quick enough to register domain names themselves, only to find later that private individuals had already obtained them. In the UK the situation was slightly different, in that laws against "passing off" already existed, so it was difficult (though not impossible) for individuals to register domain names for well-

DID YOU KNOW?
It only costs a few pounds annually to register a domain name, and it is not necessary actually to create a Website to go with it. Many companies register variants of their names simply to ensure that no one else will be able to use them in the future.

known British companies.

But you should remember that even perfectly legitimate domain names do not necessarily belong to the organizations that you may initially expect. The Website **http://www. amex.com** is not the debit card company: it is used by the American Stock Exchange; and **http://www.aa.com** is the address for American Airlines and not, as British readers may assume, the Automobile Association.

Company logo

The second thing that I check when looking at a Website is to see if it carries a recognizable company or organizational logo. This is not a foolproof method of ensuring the legitimacy of the site, of course, but it does provide further corroborating evidence. Copyright laws exist on the Internet in the same way that they exist elsewhere, and individuals cannot simply copy any material that they find on Websites; if they do, they run the risk of receiving a sharp attorney's letter telling them to cease and desist! Many companies are very strict in the use that can be made of their logos, sometimes to the extent of refusing to allow them to be used as a graphic link from other sites back to their own.

Contact details

Every site on the Web has been created by someone at some time. I am much more likely to treat a Website seriously if it provides contact details for the author or person responsible for the site. Then I know that if I have problems, either technically or with the information on the site, there is someone I can contact about them. If no contact details are given (and this happens surprisingly often), it makes me wonder what is wrong with the site, since no one is prepared to take responsibility for the data on it.

Currency

When I view a Website, I want to make sure that the data on it is current. It is usually easy to check this with a printed publication, but almost impossible to do so with a Website,

DID YOU KNOW?

You will often see discussions centered on the fact that domain names are going to run out. What is actually meant is that good domain names will run out. The potential number of different domain names that are available is: 1,075,911,801,979,990,000, 000,000,000,000,000,000,00, 000,000,000,000,000,000,000 – and that doesn't take into account any future top-level domain addresses that may be added in the future!

DID YOU KNOW?

Copyright laws apply to the Internet in the same way that they do to printed matter. If you don't have permission from the copyright holder to use an image or text, you are probably breaking the law.

unless the author gives details of when the site was last updated. If no date is given I have no way of easily checking this and am much less inclined to take the information found on the site seriously. A good Website is constantly being updated, and I would expect to find something new, altered or updated at least monthly. Any longer than this can imply that the organization is not taking the site seriously, which casts doubt on the validity of the data. (I am of course referring to data that would be expected to change regularly.)

Awards

I quite often see sites boasting of the awards which they have won, usually accompanied by a garish medal of some description. In my opinion, these are not worth the paper they are (not) printed on. Since there are no official Internet bodies, any awards are offered by individuals or companies, and it is often quite difficult to find out exactly what the criteria are for winning an award. As a result, I retain a healthy skepticism about them.

Page design

In many cases, Web page design is entirely down to an individual's personal choice, and simply because the page is displayed as red text on a green background does not automatically invalidate the information it contains. However, if an individual or organization cares about their site, they should ensure that the pages can be viewed well using any browser in any screen resolution. Anything less implies once again that they are not taking their site seriously, so I am less inclined to trust the data that I find.

Who owns a site?

If I am still in doubt I may well check to see who a particular site is registered to. Many Web-hosting companies will provide free utilities for you to check and see if a site has already been registered, and the one I generally use is *Easyspace* at **http://www.easyspace.com**. You simply input the name of the site you are interested in, and if it has been registered you can click on the option for more information and obtain details on who registered the site, their address, when the site was registered and who the contacts for technical and administrative details are.

As I have demonstrated, there are many things that need to be taken into account when assessing the authority of a site, but the experienced searcher will quickly become adept at sorting out the wheat from the chaff. However, if you are working in an unfamiliar area, it does become more difficult, and this is where virtual libraries can play an important role.

Checking against other sources

It almost goes without saying that it is worthwhile checking the information that you retrieve from a Web page with a known source of good data. It would of course be possible to check every single fact you find on one site against those you find on another, but that way lies madness. If you have to be certain about the authority of the information you are going to be using, simply choose one fact which can be quickly and easily checked against another source. If the results tally, then you can be reasonably reassured that other data on the site is accurate, and if they do not, then you may need to do a little more research to be certain that you can reliably use the information.

What is a virtual library?

Virtual libraries are called many different things: gateways, digital collections, digital libraries and cyber libraries are just a few of the terms in current use. Whatever they are called, they have certain things in common.

➤ They are collaborative ventures in which information professionals and other experts in specific subject areas pool their knowledge and experience to collate information on a specific subject.
➤ Information is checked for accuracy and authority.
➤ Their geographical position is not important – the focus is on the information contained within them rather than on which continent they are located.

➤ Data is displayed clearly and concisely, allowing for easy navigation.
➤ They are kept current.

What does a virtual library contain?

Since all virtual libraries are slightly different, it is not possible to give a complete listing of everything that you might find in one – you'll have to discover that for yourself! However, you can generally expect to find a mixture of the following:

➤ links to other Websites and resources
➤ newsletters, either about the subject area or about the virtual library itself
➤ databases of resources listed at the library, and links to databases which cover the particular subject area
➤ subject guides to provide you with more information and background in the various specialisms covered by the subject area
➤ documents (full text)
➤ lists of meetings, conferences and exhibitions
➤ information about mailing lists and newsgroups in the subject area
➤ what's new and information announcements
➤ bibliographies
➤ books in electronic format
➤ reports and papers.

When should an information professional use a virtual library?

There are almost as many reasons why you should consider using a virtual library as there are libraries! Some of the major reasons are:

➤ Virtual libraries provide authoritative, factual information.
➤ If time is short, they are a useful resource since they contain focused, appropriate information. Search engines, while useful, will often return large numbers of hits, even with very precise searches, and many of these may have

Fig. 10.1 *The "WWW Virtual Library" logo*
Courtesy of The WWW Virtual Library

limited relevance to the subject.

➤ Virtual libraries generally provide precise, accurate descriptions of information, saving time when trying to decide which resource to look at.

➤ Virtual libraries are kept current, so there should be few, if any, broken links.

➤ Virtual libraries collect subject-specific materials in one place.

➤ They provide an overview of a subject, which is useful if you have limited knowledge of that subject.

Virtual libraries currently available

The *WWW Virtual Library*

The *WWW Virtual Library* is the oldest catalog of the Web. It was begun by Tim Berners-Lee, the "founding father" of the Web, and is in fact a collection of subject-specific libraries, a list of which is available at **http://www.vlib.org.** Subject coverage runs from agriculture to West European studies, with gardening, history, sport and many other subjects in between. The libraries associated with the *WWW Virtual Library* generally display a particular logo which, although it is in the public domain and therefore can be used by anyone, has become associated with them. This is shown in Figure 10.1. Figure 10.2 shows the *WWW Virtual Library* home page at Stanford, and there is also a mirror site in the UK at **http://vlib.org.uk.**

The *WWW Virtual Library* does not exist in one single place, but is distributed around the world, individual libraries being held on different servers, maintained by different people. The central affairs of the VL are co-ordinated by a council, which took office in January 2000, and major decisions are decided by the membership at large. Consequently, the

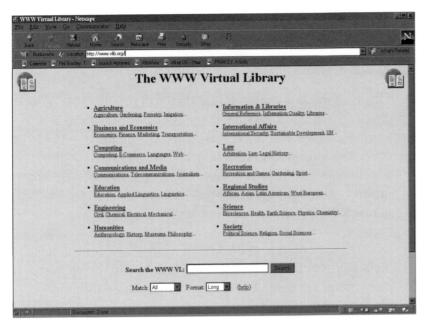

Fig. 10.2 *The "WWW Virtual Library" home page*
Courtesy of The WWW Virtual Library

information that you will find in each of the component virtual libraries differs in accordance with the subject under consideration.

The eLib Programme

eLib, the Electronic Libraries Programme at **http://www. ukoln.ac.uk/services/elib/** in conjunction with JISC at **http://www.jisc.ac.uk** was instrumental in the establishment of a number of virtual libraries, in particular a project called ROADS (Resource Organisation And Discovery in Subject-based Services), which is a confederation of virtual libraries based in the UK.

ROADS performs a number of different operations; it has produced software to enable the creation of virtual libraries, investigates methods of cross-searching between gateways, and assists in the development of indexing, cataloging and searching resources.

There are a number of different subject-specific gateways within the ROADS system; for an overview you can visit their site at **http://www.ilrt.bris.ac.uk/roads/who/**, or you may prefer just to jump in and go directly to look at

HINTS AND TIPS
Although the ROADS project has now ended, information on it is still available and is useful to read to gain a deeper understanding of how systems like this work.

some of the sites themselves.

The ROADS gateways differ in a number of significant respects from the *WWW Virtual Library*:

➤ The sites are not static, in that they offer searchable databases of manually cataloged resources. Most of the *WWW Virtual Library* has to be searched page by page to discover the information required.

➤ The subject coverage is not as wide as the *WWW Virtual Library*, although those subjects that are covered tend to be in more depth, often with over 3000 resources being cataloged.

➤ ROADS sites tend to run computerized procedures to automatically check that links are still active, and they periodically check the resources to ensure that the descriptions given are still accurate.

Other virtual libraries

Of course, not all virtual libraries are involved in the ROADS system, and a good example of an independent library (which also receives no funding) is HUMBUL, the HUManities BULletin Board at **http://www.humbul.ac/uk/**. As the name suggests, HUMBUL concentrates on the humanities, and covers subjects such as anthropology, archaeology, the classics, dictionaries, history, language and linguistics, libraries, music and religious studies, to name but a few.

The following is a list of current gateways which are associated with the eLib project, but more are being added all the time.

➤ *Agricultural Network Information Center*
  http://www.agnic.org.
➤ *Animal Omnibus*
  http://www.animalomnibus.com/
➤ *AskERIC*
  http://ericir.syr.edu/
➤ *TThe Dismal Scientist*
  http://www.economy.com/dismal/
➤ *The Eserver*
  http://eserver.org/
➤ *Contemplations from the Marianas Trench: folk Music of*

Britain, Ireland & America
http://www.contemplator.com/
➤ *Hardin MD*
http://www.lib.uiowa.edu/hardin/md
➤ *HIPPIAS: Limited Area Search of Philosophy on the Internet*
http://hippias.evansville,edu/
➤ *ICE: Internet Connection for Engineers*
http://www.englib.cornell.edu/ice/
➤ *Medieval Feminist Index*
http://www. haverford.edu/library/reference/mschaus/ mfi/mfi.html
➤ *The National Academics*
http://national-academies.org/
➤ *Scholarly Journals Diestributed Via the World Wide Web*
http://info.lib.uh.edu/wj/webjour.html
➤ *Statistical Resosurces on the Web*
http://www.lib.umich.edu/govdocs/stats.html
➤ *US News Archives on the Web*
http://www.ibiblo.org/slanews/internet/archives.html
➤ *WebElements*
http://www.ibiblo.org/slanews/internet/archives.html
➤ *YourDisctionary.com*
http://www.yourdisctionary.com/

If you wish to find more virtual libraries, a good search engine, specifically designed for this purpose, is *Alpha Search* at **http://www.calvin.edu/library/searreso/Internet/asl**; and another good collection of links to over 40 virtual libraries is *Pinakes*, a subject launchpad hosted by Heriot-Watt University at **http://www.hw.ac.uk/libWWW/ irn/pinakes/pinakes.html**.

A virtual library in action

Having looked at virtual libraries in general terms, let us now look at one in action. I've chosen to look at *BUBL*, based at **http://www.bubl.ac.uk** which is an information service designed for the UK higher-education community. However, its use is much wider than that, since it is used by academic communities in the UK and abroad, as well as by librarians, information professionals, and indeed anyone with access to

DID YOU KNOW?
When the service began in 1990, BUBL stood for BUlletin Board for Libraries, but it is now generally referred to as the BUBL Information Service.

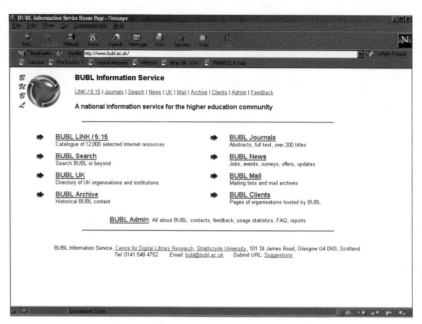

Fig. 10.3 *The "BUBL Information Service" home page*
Copyright © BUBL Information Service

the Internet. The major aim of the service is to "provide clear, fast and reliable access to selected information sources, which means no adverts, no animations, and few graphics." The home page is reproduced as Figure 10.3; as can be seen, it provides access to a very wide variety of information. Users seeking UK-oriented material can use *BUBL UK* to quickly find information on aspects of the UK such as central government, political parties, newspapers, the media, UK Web directories, academic information, hospitals, libraries, museums and so on.

BUBL LINK is a database or catalog of Internet resources of academic relevance, with each resource being evaluated, classified and cataloged before being added. It is organized by the Dewey Decimal Classification system, and can be browsed by subject or class number. The section on library and information services is arranged, in part, as follows:

020   Library and information science: general resources
020   Library and information science: departments
020   Library and information science: discussion lists
020   Library and information science: journals
020.6 Library organizations

021   Co-operation and resource sharing
023   Personnel administration
025   Operations of libraries and information centers
027.4 Public libraries
027.5 National and government libraries
027.7 University and college libraries
027.8 School libraries

Specific searches can be undertaken using the *BUBL Search* interface. The major differences between doing a search in *BUBL* rather than using a general search engine are as follows:

➤ A smaller, focused set of resources is used, reducing the number of results returned, and thereby saving time.
➤ The user obtains more information about the site, such as resource type (bibliography, index, documents, articles).
➤ The name of the author or organization responsible for each site found is immediately available.

BUBL provides users with an extraordinarily useful service, called *BUBL LINK/5:15*, which is a list of selected Internet resources covering all academic subject areas – over 12,000 in fact. The search interface is rather like *Yahoo!* in that users can choose to search in 10 major categories such as general reference, humanities, engineering and technology, the life sciences and physical sciences. Alternatively, the service also has a search facility allowing you to input search terms and match them to title, author, description or subject. Once you have located the subject that you're interested in from the major categories list, you can then focus your search more closely by choosing a more specific category and will then be presented with (usually) somewhere between 5 and 15 links to Websites that cover your interest in depth. This listing will also include a short paragraph summarizing the site, thus enabling you to visit the right site at the first attempt.

I ran a search for intelligent agents and have reproduced the results in Figure 10.4. As can be seen, this resulted in a total of eight hits when searching for subject matches. The same search when run on *AltaVista* resulted in 33,972 matches. This is perhaps not a fair comparison, since I would

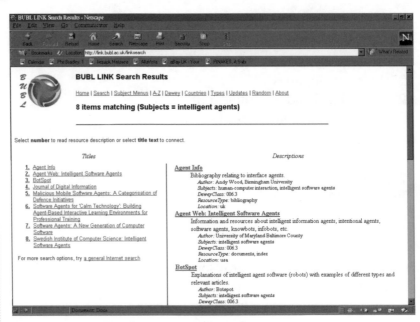

Fig. 10.4 *Results of search at "BUBL LINK 5:15"*
Copyright © BUBL Information Service

normally have been much more precise in the *AltaVista* search, but even then I would have got far too many hits and would have had to spend a lot of time visiting returned sites in order to find exactly what I wanted. Using the *BUBL* service I can rest assured that the sites found are going to be of high quality and will be appropriate to me as an information professional.

Summary

Virtual libraries and gateways are an extremely useful way of ensuring that you can limit the results of a search to a manageable number of hits that are current, informative and authoritative. Their strength lies in the fact that the resources made available have been evaluated and selected, and in the summaries, which are created by professionals who work in the area in which the library operates. Paradoxically, however, this is also their weakness, since this human intervention takes time and a lot of voluntary effort, which may mean that the resources listed are not as current as they should be. Nonetheless, a virtual library is always a good way to begin exploring a subject area, safe in the knowledge that the information retrieved will always be of high quality.

URLs mentioned in this chapter

http://www.philb.com
http://www.amex.com
http://www.aa.com
http://www.easyspace.com
http://www.vlib.org
http://vlib.org.uk
http://www.ukoln.ac.uk/services/elib/
http://www.jisc.ac.uk
http://www.ilrt.bris.ac.uk/roads/who/
http://www.agnic.org.
http://www.animalomnibus.com/
http://ericir.syr.edu/
http://www.economy.com/dismal/
http://eserver.org/
http://www.contemplator.com/
http://www.lib.uiowa.edu/hardin/md
http://hippias.evansville,edu/
http://www.englib.cornell.edu/ice/
http://www.
    haverford.edu/library/reference/mschaus/mfi/mfi.html
http://national-academies.org/
http://info.lib.uh.edu/wj/webjour.html
http://www.lib.umich.edu/govdocs/stats.html
http://www.ibiblo.org/slanews/internet/archives.html
http://www.ibiblo.org/slanews/internet/archives.html
http://www.yourdisctionary.com/
http://www.calvin.edu/library/searreso/Internet/asl
http://www.hw.ac.uk/libWWW/irn/pinakes/pinakes. html
http://www.humbul.ac.uk/
http://www.bubl.ac.uk

Part 2

Becoming an expert searcher

11

Intelligent agents

Introduction

In this chapter we'll look at intelligent agents in some detail. As you will see, intelligent agents are a logical step forward in the process of searching and retrieving information. There are a number of different types of intelligent agent – some free, some commercial, some that can be downloaded and some that can be used directly from a Website. I will focus on some of the ways in which they can be used, and give examples of some of those that I find particularly useful.

What is an intelligent agent?

Probably the best way of answering this question is to provide you with the analogy of a librarian or other information professional. Imagine that you are in a situation where you are an end-user seeking some data. You go into the library and ask the librarian for the information that you need about your chosen subject. The librarian goes away and finds information that may or may not be exactly what you are looking for, so you keep some material and discard the rest. The librarian can take a note of what you keep and what you decide not to use, and can then go away and redo the search for you, returning a few minutes later with more information, which more closely matches your inquiry. The librarian has learned, from looking at what you find useful and what you don't, the exact type of information you are interested in, and this results in the retrieval of new, more appropriate information. This of course is very helpful, but our librarian

HINTS AND TIPS
If you have to provide a current awareness service, consider using an intelligent agent; this will save you a lot of time as you will not need to keep re-running searches – the intelligent agent will do that for you.

is even more efficient than that, because the next time you go into the library you may find a pile of new books and magazines waiting for you with the latest up-to-date information on your subject.

In essence, this is exactly what an intelligent agent (or to give it the name it is often known by, a robot) can do for you. You can ask it for information on a particular subject and it can retrieve information from a variety of different sources, allowing you then to define more closely what you want before telling it to go and search further. It can also work on your behalf to retrieve more information in the future without your having to do anything else, thus keeping you nicely up to date.

Consequently, an intelligent search agent should fulfill a number of criteria:

➤ **It should be able to operate without direct intervention of human beings**
It should not be necessary to tell an agent exactly what to do at every step of the search process; it should be able to work out for itself what it does and where it goes to obtain information for you.

➤ **It should be able to exert some control over its actions**
Once again, the searcher should not need to tell the agent exactly what to do. Once it has been informed of the type of information that is required, it should be able to seek out appropriate information from appropriate resources.

➤ **It needs to be able to interact with human beings via some sort of interface**
Obviously you will need to tell an agent what to do, so there has to be an interface, but hopefully this interface should be straightforward and easy to use.

➤ **Agents need to be able to exchange messages between each other and other interfaces**
The agent needs to be able to contact other resources (such as search engines or other agents) to exchange and pool knowledge.

➤ **They need to be aware of their environment and have to be able to respond to changes as they occur**
An agent should know what it should be doing (either with or without direct commands), should be able to look for information as required, and should keep itself up to date by, for example, downloading a new list of search engines or updates to existing lists.

➤ **They should be able to act without direct commands by taking the initiative**
While it is of course necessary to tell an agent what you want done, it should then be able just to get on with the job, such as re-running a search every few days for you and making you aware of the results.

Search engines or intelligent agents?

As we have seen elsewhere, and as you have doubtless already discovered for yourself, although there are advantages to search engines there are an equal number of disadvantages. A search engine will in the main simply do exactly as it is told and will return pages to you that match your search criteria, but it will have no way of knowing if the information on the pages has any "real" value to you. Search engines will also rank pages according to a set of algorithms that have been decided upon by programmers. Now, without wishing to denigrate programmers, they don't always know what is the best way to rank results, leading to a situation where a page that is of particular interest to you is hidden way down in the list of returned results – you as the user have no control (other than by deciding on terms in your initial search strategy) over the way in which this is done. Search engines will also return results listing pages that no longer exist (since until they revisit a site they won't know that a page has been deleted), causing frustration for the user. As we shall see, intelligent agents can overcome all of these problems, as well as some others besides!

However, there are disadvantages to agents as well. So that the intelligent agent can understand what you are interested in, and focus its search more closely, you have to spend quite a lot of time with it initially – "training" it to find the good

DID YOU KNOW?
Most of the time you spend on the Web you are pulling information down from servers around the world onto your computer. At your command your browser connects to the remote server hosting the page and copies the data back onto your hard disk to display for you. This obviously requires work on your part, and the page remains static, in that the browser obtained the copy of the page that was available at the time. "Push" technology works slightly differently, in that the remote server takes responsibility for updating the page and pushing it through to you on a regular basis without your having to refresh the page for yourself.

material and ignore the bad. Equally, you are reliant on the agent to look in the right places. You might be able to find some useful information for yourself by searching the Web, but if the agent doesn't know about a particular source, it is not going to be able to use it when looking for appropriate data. Consequently, there will almost always be a degree of uncertainty as to whether you've got all the information that is available to you. On the other hand, you could equally argue that, as long as the agent (or indeed the search engine) has found the right source, it doesn't much matter if there are other sites that have been overlooked!

A further problem is that an intelligent agent is of little use if you want to do a "quick and dirty" search to start you off. In the time that it might take to train an agent, you could have run a search, found some information in the right area which matches your query, passed the data on to your user and even considered where to go for lunch! Computers are wonderful at number crunching, but they fail miserably when you need an intuitive approach. However, if you are running a current awareness service, an intelligent agent may well be the best approach to take. It will present you with a variety of results, and you can then just pick the best, saving you the time and energy it would otherwise have taken to run the search once a month, or even once a day.

Intelligent agents on the Web

Having discussed some of the background issues, let's now take a closer look at how these intelligent agents have been implemented on the Web, and the ways in which you can make use of them. As you would expect, there are a variety of different approaches, and I'll take them one at a time. We'll start by taking a look at one or two implementations that don't have much use in the day-to-day world of the information professional, but which will give you a clearer idea of how these things work. Besides, they are quite amusing!

Intelligent agents that learn from your preferences

There are a variety of agents that will learn from your likes and dislikes and will then attempt to make suggestions based upon your preferences. There are several nice examples of these on the Internet at the moment, and in particular I like *Alexandria Digital Literature* at **http://www.alexlit.com/**. This agent (called Hypatia) asks you to rate a number of books that you have read, and once you have input data rating a minimum of 40 titles, it will be able to suggest other titles that it thinks you would probably enjoy reading. I tried the system out, and it seemed very top heavy with science fiction titles, but there is an option of choosing your own favorite authors and rating those as well. I was quite impressed with the results that were returned to me. If you don't like this version, you may wish to explore *The Readers Robot,* which can be found at **http://www.tnrdlib. bc.ca/rr.html.** Both of these agents are really designed to provide you with fiction titles rather than non-fiction, hence my comment earlier about little professional value (unless perhaps you happen to be choosing books for the public library).

The *Amazon* bookshop at **http://www.amazon.com** has a facility which will update you every time books are added to its catalog that match your own particular interests. It is pushing a point rather a lot to call it an "intelligent agent," since it is very basic, but having said that, it is a useful feature of their Website.

If books are not your thing, you might like to try out movies at the *Moviecritic* at **http://www.moviecritic.com/**, which works in pretty much the same way.

Moving towards the Internet now, if intelligent agents can choose books or films for you, they can also find Web pages that will be of use for you. The *Web Bird* finds pages that it thinks you will like, based on a list which you supply of pages/sites that you already like or find useful. Unfortunately, the *Web Bird* (at **http://ai.iit.nrc.ca/II_public/WebBird/ tryIt.html**) only works via e-mail. It does help if you can supply a lot of Web pages for it to work on – I only tried four and didn't have any luck with it, so I'd recommend you to have a list of about 10 URLs that you can feed to it.

All of these agents work on the same principle, that of like minds. You are asked to rate books or movies and the agent can match your likes and dislikes against those of people who have already gone through the process. Therefore, using movies as the example, an intelligent agent will correlate the fact that many people who like the Star Wars series of films also like the Star Trek series. If you indicate that you like Star Wars but you have not seen any of the Star Trek films, it can recommend one, fairly certain in the knowledge that you will actually enjoy it.

Intelligent search engines

It's likely that you'll find agents such as the ones mentioned above to be quite addictive and time-consuming, so I won't give you any additional examples or you'll never get any work done! Now let's turn to agents that will search for you. There are many examples of this type of agent, so I'll simply concentrate on one or two; if they are not to your liking you might want to take a look at *Botspot* at **http://www.botspot. com/s-search.htm**, which lists well over 100 of them.

Copernic at **http://www.copernic.com** has a number of search agents available, from free versions (with limited functionality) to commercial products. *Copernic 2001 basic* is the free version, which can be downloaded directly from their site. The agent gives instant access to some of the best search engines on the Internet, such as *AltaVista*, *Excite*, *HotBot*, *InfoSeek*, *Lycos*, *WebCrawler* and *Yahoo!* – in total, over 80 search engines in seven major categories. Once the program has been downloaded and installed, the user has a search screen similar to the one seen in Figure 11.1.

Seven categories are available for searching – six defaults and one that can be chosen (mine being searching UK Web pages), although this restriction doesn't exist with the commercial versions. Users can run free-text searches of their choice and *Copernic* simultaneously passes the search out to 10 major search engines and displays the results on screen, including details of the site, its URL, its relevance, search engines that located a specific Web page, and a summary of the pages returned. These can then be viewed via a browser, downloaded for later viewing, translated if required, and searches can also be scheduled to be run again at a specified point in the future. Duplicate Web pages are removed from the results, and the keywords are highlighted, making it reasonably easy to locate the page(s) that interest you quickly. Dead links are eliminated and searches can also be refined quickly and easily.

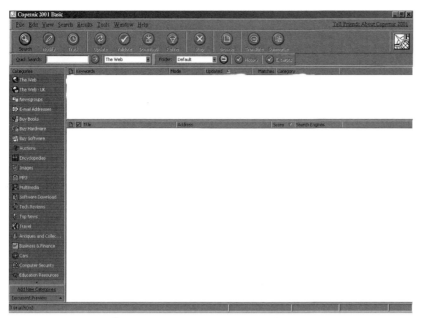

Fig. 11.1　The "Copernic 2001" search interface
© Copernic Technologies Inc.

Commercial versions of the product (*Copernic Plus* and *Copernic Pro*) extend the existing capabilities of the product to include e-mail notification of new documents, an automatic refine facility, and access to over 1000 search engines.

Another product which works in a similar way to *Copernic* is *LexiBot*™ (found at **http://www.lexibot.com/**), which was previously called *Mata Hari*. Once again, *LexiBot* is downloaded onto your system and it can then be used to search up to 600 search engines in one go, making it almost a "multi-meta-search engine." Figure 11.2 shows the *LexiBot* search screen during a query for "intelligent agents."

Once the search has been run, the pages can be viewed in a browser or as text. Searches can be simple text queries or structured (Boolean) queries, with an option to enforce strict Boolean adherence, while other options allow for wildcards and phrases. Once *LexiBot* has delivered a set of results, these can be manipulated, annotated, saved and reranked, giving the agent more information about your search, and ensuring that if it is used to rerun the search the results should be more relevant.

One final agent that helps to illustrate the power of these

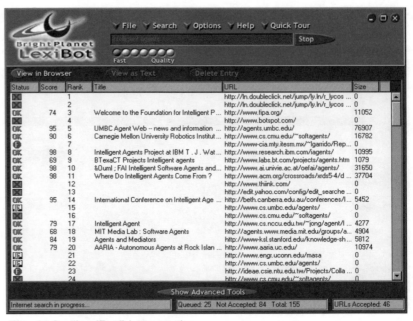

Fig. 11.2 *"LexiBot" in operation*
*Copyright © 2000–2001 BrightPlanet (**www.brightplanet.com**)*

DID YOU KNOW?

The *Alexa* database is over 10 terabytes in size. One tera byte is a million megabytes or 1,099,511, 627,776 bytes in size. In other words – an awful lot of information!

utilities is *Alexa* at **http://www.alexa.com**. *Alexa* is a free download which can be installed into more recent versions of browsers, and when you visit a Website *Alexa* can quickly locate related links, provide you with various shopping tools with a price comparison, Website traffic statistics and contact information. Figure 11.3 illustrates the *Alexa Snapshot* product used with the Netscape browser when viewing the *Libraries for the Future* Website. Installation of the product for Netscape is as simple as dragging a link to the toolbar and clicking on it as appropriate when visiting a Web page; it has to be the quickest and easiest installation of a product that I have ever done! Other options to enhance the *Alexa* capabilities are available for download and installation into the user's browser.

Intelligent newspapers

An easy way to see how intelligent agents work is to look at some of the personalized newspapers that are currently available on the Web. These are appearing quite regularly now, a nd are an extremely good way of keeping up to date in subject areas that are of interest to you. As you might expect,

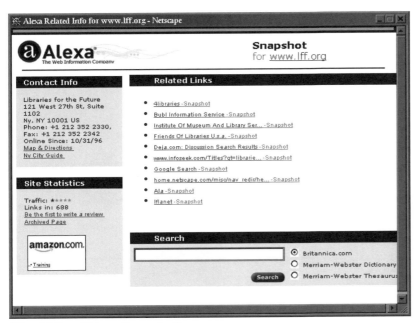

Fig. 11.3 "Alexa Snapshot"
© Alexa Internet

some are more intelligent than others. The majority of these newspapers allow you to define broad areas of interest, such as world news, politics, weather, business briefings and so on. Some also allow you to list a historical fact of the day, your horoscope or even your favorite cartoon strip!

Each time you visit your intelligent newspaper it will update itself for you, providing you with the latest news in the subject categories that you have chosen. Consequently, the newspaper will ensure that you get to see new breaking stories, latest stocks and shares information, and so on. In order to do this, the newspaper will visit a variety of different resources on your behalf – Websites, news sources and so on – and will either display these on the screen in their entirety, or give you the headline, with a link to the source, thus allowing you to click on the link to read the story.

A good example of a personalized newspaper can be found at *CRAYON*, or *CReAte Your Own Newspaper* at **http://www.crayon.net.** Figure 11.4 shows you a recent copy of *The Phil Bradley Times*.

This personalized newspaper took about five minutes to create, simply by choosing the subject areas that I was inter-

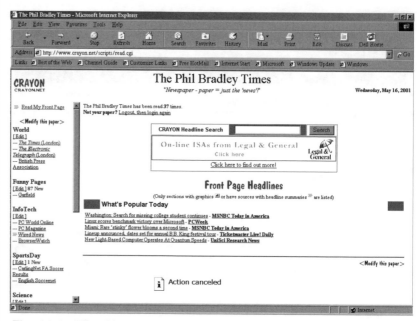

Fig. 11.4 *"The Phil Bradley Times" at "CRAYON"*

ested in from a large list of general and specific subject areas. I then had to decide on the way in which I wanted the paper to be laid out on the screen (as you can see, I created it as a frames page, with summary information on the left and the main body of the text in the right-hand frame). I then bookmarked the page, so that when I return to it in the future it will recognize who I am and dynamically refresh the page, updating the information contained within it.

Another interesting news resource is the *NewsTracker* provided by *Excite* at **http://nt.excite.com/**. The service is free, although you do have to register with *Excite* before you can start to use it. Once you have registered, you are prompted to give a name to the subject that you're interested in tracking, and then provide keywords which should or should not be included in your search. If appropriate *NewsTracker* will suggest other terms for you as well. Once you have decided on your keywords the utility will then search across a wide range of news sources to provide you with appropriate stories. Most of these resources are American, but by no means all of them. Once you have viewed a story you can indicate if it is relevant to you, allowing the *NewsTracker* service to refine its searches to bring you more focused material. *Excite* also offers (in common with many other search engines) a more generalized news service where you can once again specify subject areas of interest and be kept informed about current events. (Personalized sources of information via search engines will be discussed in more detail later in this chapter.)

One final example of intelligent agents in this category is the *Infogate* product at **http://www.infogate.com/**. Once again, this is a utility which is downloaded onto your desktop, allowing you to personalize the information you receive in a number of ways. Firstly, you can select news sources such as news, stocks, sports, weather and so on. *Infogate* aggregates the content from information sources such as *The New York Times*, *CNN*, *Marketwatch*, *Reuters*, *CBS Sportsline*, *E! Online* and more. Once *Infogate* discovers a news story that will interest you, the data is delivered to your desktop, pager or even cell phone!

Traditional search engines and intelligent agents

So far we have looked at intelligent agents that are stand-alone products – that is to say, products which are designed to work by themselves without being integrated into other, existing products. However, search engines are also trying to provide users with intelligent agents by integrating them into existing products. The organizations which run search engines are constantly looking for ways in which to increase their user base, and as a result this concept is very appealing. Since these engines have large databases available to them, the inclusion of an intelligent agent is a natural next step. The search engine can interrogate a user request and then provide either an updating service or suggestions as to other potentially useful sites. We've already seen this with a service such as *Ask Jeeves* at **http://www.aj.com**, for example. However, others are doing similar work, so let's take a look at some examples.

My Yahoo! is one of the stable of products produced by the Yahoo! Corporation. It allows you to create your own user profile based on the *Yahoo!* system of subject headings and current events. The basics of the system are quite simple; you visit *Yahoo!* at **http://www.yahoo.com**, input details about yourself (user name, password and so on), and choose from a number of broad categories (such as business, entertainment or a stock portfolio) and subdivisions beneath those. These then form the basis of your personalized page.

Yahoo! is then able to create a user profile based on this information. It can then produce pages "on the fly" (that is to say, dynamically create them for users), and display news and current events information covering your areas of interest. If you enjoy baseball, want to know what the weather is like in Florida, or want to check the winning numbers in the California lottery, *My Yahoo!* can do this for you. If you also need to be kept informed about stock prices and the latest corporate takeover in the telecommunications world, a simple mouse click to take you to the business section of your pages keeps you instantly in touch. Figure 11.5 illustrates a sample *My Yahoo!* page. As you can see, it is possible to get very quick access to sections such as Top Stories from Reuters, World from Reuters, Business from Reuters, various portfolios, sporting results and so on.

My Yahoo! also allows you to store frequently run searches and offers a news clipping facility that enables you to create your own searches, which you can store and run whenever you wish, to keep you fully up to date with what is happening in your area(s) of interest. You can specify the name of the search, and there is an edit feature that allows you to add or change the search terms that are being used. Once you have created the searches required, a click on the "Finished" button sends the details back to your personalized page, and the searches can then be run whenever you wish.

My Yahoo! does not bring information directly to your desktop, since you have to visit the site in order to obtain the new information, but you can always bookmark the page and revisit whenever you wish; the content is continually updated, so unless you're a news junkie and are checking every couple of minutes, you should always find new information available.

If you do not like the way in which *Yahoo!* has implemented its service, I would suggest looking at other search engines. Many of them have already introduced such a service – we've already seen that *Excite* has done so, while *Lycos*

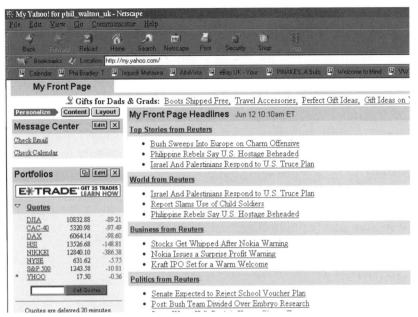

Fig. 11.5 *"My Yahoo!" front page*
© 2001 Yahoo! Inc.

offers *My Lycos* and *HotBot* offers *my.HotBot* at **http://www. hotbot.lycos.co.uk/index.html?coomo.x=1** (I suspect that a trend is already evident in the naming convention!).

The effect of intelligent agents on the information profession

At first sight, intelligent agents may appear to threaten the traditional role of the information provider. After all, if a piece of software can be trained to locate appropriate information for the end-user and deliver it direct to the screen, how can the professional hope to compete?

However, I do not feel that the situation is actually as clear-cut as this. Intelligent agents are still at a very early phase in their development, and they can still provide inexplicable results. For example, I trained one agent to provide me with all the latest information on the football team that I follow, and the agent returned with a series of results, most of which dealt with Formula One motor racing! So the term "intelligent" is still something of a misnomer, and it is going to be a long time before agents are actually able to carry out complex searches with a high degree of accuracy.

HINTS AND TIPS

When using an intelligent agent, provide it with as much information as you possibly can – then it will be able to focus on appropriate sites much more quickly.

Furthermore, in order to ensure that the agent produces high-quality results, considerable "training" has to take place. The intelligent newspapers can only really provide a rough guide to overall areas of interest, and intelligent search engines require a lot of work to produce a tightly focused set of results. They are very time-consuming, and it is unlikely that they will appeal to busy end-users who simply want results quickly. They do have a very important role to play within an information service, however, and may prove to be an important addition in the information professional's armory when it comes to providing a current awareness or selective dissemination service.

Summary

The benefits of intelligent agents are clear:
➤ The agents reduce the time taken searching the Internet for information.
➤ They can re-run searches for you on a regular basis.
➤ They overcome the problem of sorting out the new material from a mass of Web pages which have already been looked at in the past.
➤ The material that they retrieve is almost always going to be relevant.
➤ The user does not need to learn about search techniques and methods, or explore the intricacies of browsing and monitoring newsgroups.
➤ If a company is running an intranet it does not need to institute complicated methods of ensuring that the employees see important documents or information, since the agents will immediately inform them of new data as soon as it is made available.
➤ Virtual communities of users can easily be created, allowing enhanced sharing of information.
➤ Updated information can be displayed on a personalized Web page for you, allowing immediate access to the data itself via hypertext links.
➤ Agents continue to work even when you have gone home for the night, preparing updated information ready for viewing when you arrive at work the next morning.

➤ Intelligent agents allow you to set up a number of profiles which may be subject-specific or designed for particular individuals or groups.

URLs mentioned in this chapter

http://bots.internet.com/search/s-chat.htm
http://www.alexlit.com/
http://www.tnrdlib.bc.ca/rr.html
http://www.amazon.com
http://www.moviecritic.com/
http//ai.iit.nrc.ca/II_public/WebBird/tryIt.html
http://www.botspot.com/s-search.htm
http://www.copernic.com
http://www.lexibot.com/
http://www.brightplanet.com
http://www.alexa.com
http://www.crayon.net
http://nt.excite.com/
http://www.infogate.com/
http://www.aj.com
http://www.yahoo.com
http://www.hotbot.lycos.co.uk/index.html?coomo.x=1

12

Usenet newsgroups and mailing lists

Introduction

The Internet is useful for many things, but perhaps it is best
used for communication, either between individuals or
groups of people. E-mail was the first implementation of
this, but it is limited in what it can provide. What was also
required was a method of passing information between
groups of people, all of whom shared the same interests,
whether academic or personal. Two methods have been introduced, usenet newsgroups and mailing lists. This chapter
discusses the similarities and differences between them,
how to make use of them, and the advantages that they can
give you as an information professional.

Usenet newsgroups

I expect that you have heard of usenet newsgroups, though
you may have heard them described as any of the following:
usenet, newsgroups, netnews, discussion groups, or just
news. For simplicity, I'll refer to them as newsgroups, but it
is worth pointing out that, while they do carry a lot of news
and current events information, that is not their only purpose. Newsgroups initially started life as far back as 1980,
when two students in North Carolina established a method
of transferring up to a dozen messages per day from one
machine to another using something called UUCP (UNIX
to UNIX Copy). These messages could be read by all the
users who logged onto the system, and they could respond to
the messages by posting their own, which would be copied

back to the other machine.

Over the course of time this system was expanded; because the messages dealt with different topics, a hierarchy was introduced, allowing people to post to specific newsgroups, to ensure that users did not have to wade through all the messages just to find the two or three which interested them. Newsgroups have become an ever-expanding area of the Internet – today there are about 100,000 newsgroups, and the posts to newsgroups add up to over 6 gigabytes per day. This has been doubling every year, and there are now probably as many as 50,000,000 people who participate in newsgroups. Usenet is now the largest public-information resource in the world and it is estimated that it is up to four times the size of the Web.

The method used to send newsgroup messages (commonly referred to as posts or postings) around the world is quite simple: a user posts a message to a particular newsgroup, usually using a piece of software called a newsreader (although it is now possible to post messages directly from the Web). This message is sent onwards to their Internet service provider's news server. The news server in turn copies the messages it has received to other news servers around the world, thus allowing other users to log onto their provider's news server, download the post and read it. They can then, if they choose, respond to the posts that interest them, and the whole process starts again. This is generally referred to as "propagation," and as you can see, it is continual, with people seeing posts, responding to them, having them copied around the world and so on. As with most things to do with the Internet, it is a 24-hour-a-day, 365-days-of-the-year activity.

I mentioned earlier that newsgroups are split into hierarchies, and a newsgroup name is composed of several different elements separated by dots. There is what is known as the "big seven" hierarchy, and the top level of these seven subject areas are as follows:

➤ **comp.** topics related to computing
➤ **misc.** miscellaneous topics that don't sit anywhere else in the hierarchy
➤ **news.** topics that relate to the Internet as a whole
➤ **rec.** recreational subjects such as hobbies, sports, the arts

DID YOU KNOW?
1 gigabyte is the equivalent of 1,000 400-page novels.

and so on

➤ **sci.** anything to do with scientific subjects
➤ **soc.** social newsgroups, both social interaction and social interests
➤ **talk.** which generally covers political issues.

Postings to these newsgroups are generally propagated to all news servers around the world, but there are also other newsgroups that are only of interest to particular regions, or that are regarded as rather more frivolous than the big seven. Examples of these are:

➤ **alt.** alternative, often controversial, subjects
➤ **bionet.** subjects of interest to biologists
➤ **uk.** subjects which may be of interest to people based in, or interested in, the UK.

There are a large number of other groups as well – these are just a few examples. Later in this chapter I'll explain how you can get a full list of newsgroups and choose the ones that you may find useful. For now, however, let's look a little further into the way that a newsgroup is named, with a few examples:

comp.infosystems.www.authoring.html
comp.os.ms-windows.apps.utilities.win95
misc.education
misc.misc
news.admin.censorship
news.announce.newusers
rec.pets.cats.health+behav
rec.skiing.resorts.europe
sci.physics.fusion
sci.space.shuttle
soc.culture.swiss
soc.history.war.us-civil-war
talk.abortion
talk.politics.mideast
uk.local.london
uk.media.tv.misc
alt.drugs
alt.books.iain-banks

You can see from the above examples (which were not entirely drawn at random; I have taken some of these groups myself!) that there is little by the way of a structure to the groups. Almost the only thing I can say is that they start from the general and move to the specific, but otherwise there is little overall consistency to be found. One of the reasons for this is that there is not a great deal of control over the establishment of a newsgroup, although there is a set procedure that must be adhered to in the creation of a newsgroup in the big seven, which requires that a proposition must be made and voted upon. In general terms, however, anyone can set up a newsgroup if enough people think that it is a good idea.

Most newsgroups are entirely open, which is to say that anyone can post a message to them, and although these postings are supposed to be "on topic" to the group in question, this does not always happen. Most newsgroups do, however, have a charter, which is a statement defining what sort of posts are appropriate to the group. A small number of newsgroups are "moderated," which means that, before a post is made available to news servers around the world, someone checks the message for content, validity and so on, and will only clear it for propagation if it satisfies the criteria which have previously been established.

Many newsgroups also have a FAQ, or Frequently Asked Questions list, which lists common questions and answers that people have posted to the newsgroup in the past. They can be a very useful source of information, and are usually posted about once every two weeks. A good place to get a list of FAQs is **http://www.faq.org**, and for a list of (and links to) FAQs that deal specifially with usenet you should visit **http://www.faq.org/faqs/usenet/**.

The value of newsgroups to information professionals

The posts that you find in newsgroups are an eclectic mixture of fact, fiction, rumor, advertisements and opinion. Most newsgroups are not moderated, so anyone can post anything that they like to them. In most cases posts are on-topic (that is to say, they are relevant to the subject area of the newsgroup), but sometimes people will "spam" news-

HINTS AND TIPS

Only subscribe to a small number of newsgroups in one go until you find out how busy they are, otherwise you may come in the next day to find thousands of posts waiting to be read!

DID YOU KNOW?

FAQ is usually pronounced to rhyme with "back," but you may also hear it spelled out as F-A-Q.

DID YOU KNOW?

No one can say for certain why the term "spam" became used for inappropriate postings. However, it seems likely that it is related to the Monty Python Spam sketch, in which Spam is in every item on the menu, and it is impos-sible to order anything without having at least some of it included in the meal.

DID YOU KNOW?

If you do receive UCE, don't respond to it: that simply tells the spammer that they have found an active e-mail address, and rather than getting less spam you wil receive an awful lot more!

groups with inappropriate posts. Consequently, it can take some time to sort out the useful information from the non-sense that gets posted. This depends on the number of posts a newsgroup gets every day; some low-volume newsgroups will only get two or three posts in an average day, while other newsgroups, especially some in the **comp.** hierarchy, will get over 500 posts per day.

However, it is worthwhile stressing that there is a lot of useful information to be gained from different newsgroups – the bug in the original Intel Pentium chip was reported to appropriate newsgroups, and the discussion which then took place encouraged Intel to respond to the problem quickly. Many businesses such as Microsoft, Blockbuster Video and Apple regularly monitor newsgroups, and are increasingly using them as a first-line method of communi-cating with users.

Individuals both pose and answer questions in newsgroups, debates take place, information is shared, new information is made available to each group's user community, and details on new Websites, conferences and exhibitions are regularly posted. Consequently, although the data held in newsgroups is often more opinion than fact, it can be a very useful place to begin researching a subject. Indeed, when I was writing this book, one of the first places where I looked for informa-tion on intelligent agents was in newsgroups, and I got some high-quality data, as well as lists of Websites to visit.

One word of warning here, I'm afraid. If you post to newsgroups, within a short space of time you will begin to get unsolicited commercial e-mails (UCE for short) offering anything from the chance to get rich quickly through to cures for baldness. This is because unscrupulous companies skim newsgroups for e-mail addresses, which they then sell on to other people who send out UCE. There is very little you can do about this, and although some people alter their e-mail addresses when posting to newsgroups, this is a poor solution at best.

Reading newsgroups

Having whetted your appetite for newsgroups, I'll now explain how you can use them. There are basically three ways of doing this: general search engines, Web-based utilities and software packages.

General search engines

In the first edition of this book I was able to give some details on those general search engines that provided searchers with an option to search usenet instead of the Web. However, virtually all of these engines have now discontinued this service – I suspect because the volume of material simply grew too large for them to cope with. It is therefore unlikely that you will find a general search engine that offers this service any longer, although it is always possible that you may strike lucky, or your favorite search engine decides to reintroduce the service, so it is worth keeping your eyes open, just in case!

Web-based utilities

On the Web, probably the best-known utility for searching newsgroups is a search engine that used to be called *Deja News*. This has now been taken over by the *Google* search engine at **http://groups.google.com/**. At the time of writing (May 2001), this service is still in Beta test, so when you visit, you may well find the functionality and interface have changed. It is a very specialized search engine, because all it does is to search newsgroups for you; it doesn't search the Web as *AltaVista* does, for example.

The opening screen of *Google Groups* is shown in Figure 12.1. *Google Groups* is one of the most powerful and sophisticated search engines on the Web. You can input your search terms directly into the Find box, and the search engine will attempt to find all references to the requested information across all the newsgroups.

The basic interface is very simple and straightforward to use: you can simply type in the words that you are interested in locating, and *Google* will return a list of newsgroup postings that include the word(s) you were interested in, together with a list of newsgroups that it feels are particularly appropriate to your search. The details on each post will include brief details on the thread, when it was posted, to which group and by which individual. It is also possible to read the

DID YOU KNOW?

A 'thread' is created when someone writes a post, another person responds to it and so on. The series of messages is generally referred to as a "thread" and is an easy way to follow a particular discussion.

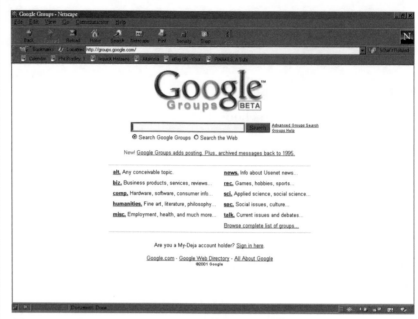

Fig. 12.1 *The "Google Groups" search interface*
Google Brand Features are trademarks of Google, Inc.

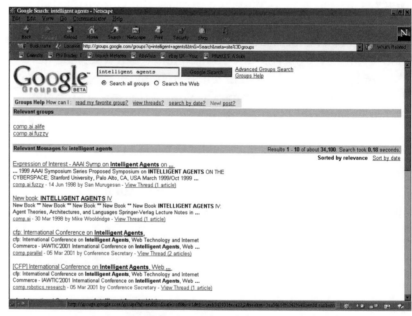

Fig. 12.2 *"Google Groups" result for "intelligent agents"*
Google Brand Features are trademarks of Google, Inc.

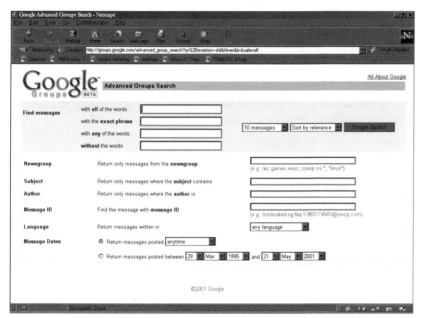

Fig. 12.3 *"Google Groups" advanced search feature*
Google Brand Features are trademarks of Google, Inc.

"thread" of messages for that particular post. You can see an example of this in Figure 12.2, which shows the first few results from a search I ran on "intelligent agents."

As you would expect, as well as individual words, you can use phrase searches (using the double quotes), and choose to include words using the "+" symbol, or exclude words using the "-" symbol.

Google Groups has an advanced function, and you can see the interface screen for this reproduced in Figure 12.3. Once you have got used to searching for newsgroup posts, the advanced search features will make a lot of sense, and will allow you to search much more quickly and effectively. As well as searching for messages that include/exclude specific text, it is possible to search in a particular group, for a particular subject line, author, message ID, language or posts written during a specific time period.

The information given is not as extensive as might be wished, but there is a limit to the amount of information that can be displayed on the screen. However, it is the matter of a few moments to click on the subject heading and display the full posting on the screen. An example of this step is shown

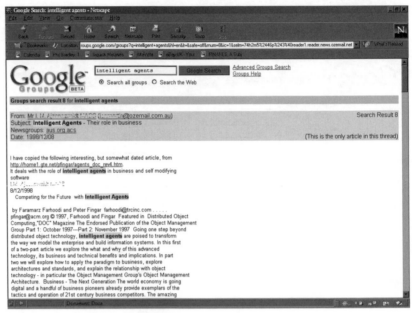

Fig. 12.4 *A "Google Groups" search for 'intelligent agents'*
Google Brand Features are trademarks of Google, Inc.

in Figure 12.4 (I've disguised the name of the individual who originally posted the question for the sake of privacy).

As you can see, there are a variety of different options available to you from this screen, and a good understanding of them will ensure that searching for information becomes even faster and more effective. When you view the posting, any URLs contained within it will be displayed as an active link, which is very useful, as you can simply click on the link and go directly to the appropriate Web page. In my opinion, this is one of the strongest features of *Google Groups*, as it really does speed up locating useful sites to visit.

Options are available to allow you to move back to a previous article, on to the next article in the thread, or to view the thread in its entirety. This is useful because it allows quick scanning in order to find answers to particular questions, or to follow a particular line of discussion.

Google Groups also encourages interaction, and it is possible to subscribe to the particular newsgroup, to post articles to the group or to e-mail the poster directly.

One final very valuable feature is the opportunity to view the posting profile of the author of the post that is being viewed. There are a number of reasons why this is useful: it allows you to identify people who are expert in a particular area, to locate lost friends or colleagues, and to track what individuals are saying and doing on newsgroups. There is of course a privacy issue involved here, but *Google Groups* does have a policy whereby posters can ensure that their postings are not archived.

Reading and posting to newsgroups can take up a frightening amount of time, so if you connect to the Internet using a dial-up modem connection, this might become an expensive way of reading newsgroups. To give you a quick example, I currently subscribe to about 20 newsgroups, and I spend at least one hour a day reading and responding to posts. If I had to do all this with an online connection I would very quickly run into financial problems, and this is where offline newsreaders become very important.

HINTS AND TIPS
Remember that most of the information you will retrieve from newsgroups is opinions, rather than facts, so be caref-ul of just relying on such information; check other sources as well.

Offline newsreaders

A possible solution to the problem of online costs is to make use of an offline newsreader. The utilities work in a similar fashion to *Google Groups*, in that you are able to obtain a list of all of the newsgroups, decide on the ones that are of interest and subscribe to them. The difference is in how the information is delivered. You log onto the Internet and start the offline newsreader, which connects to the Internet service provider and downloads all the new posts onto the local hard disk. (Offline newsreaders can usually also be configured to just downloading the subject headings.)

You are then able to read the postings offline at leisure, and can take as much time as you wish to write responses to posts, check any information and so on. Once you are happy with the responses you have written, you can log back onto the Internet and the offline reader will send the postings to the news server.

There are a great many different offline newsreaders available, and a comprehensive list of them can be found at **http://www.yahoo.com/Computers_and_Internet/ Software/Internet/Usenet**. They all work in a similar fashion; the one that I'll concentrate on here is called *Forte Free Agent*, which can be downloaded from **http://www.**

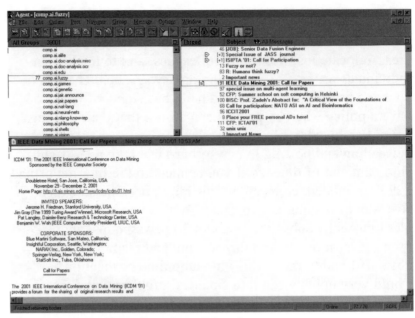

Fig. 12.5 *The "Forte Free Agent" interface*
Copyright © Forte, 2001

forteinc.com. It is simple and fast to use, and – as the name implies – it is also free, although there is a commercial version, *Agent 1.8*, which has greater functionality.

The main screen is shown in Figure 12.5. The screen is divided into three main windows: subscribed groups, subject headings, and the text of the selected article.

Free Agent is quick to configure, in that all you need to do is to give it the address of your Internet service provider's news server. It then visits the server and downloads a list of all the newsgroups the news server takes; if the ISP takes a full news feed, this may take some time, since *Free Agent* has to obtain a list of tens of thousands of newsgroups for you.

You can then browse the list of newsgroups and select the ones you are interested in receiving. *Free Agent* can then go online and download a list of subject headers for you. You can then choose (simply by clicking on the header) to retrieve the whole article there and then to read – or if you prefer, you can do this offline, marking the articles you are interested in. When you next log on, *Free Agent* can download these articles to your hard disk, and you can read them later at your leisure.

Free Agent, in common with other newsreaders, will allow

you to follow particular threads, post your own articles or responses to others, and download images and display them on the screen for you.

Mailing lists

Mailing lists (also called discussion lists or listservs) are very similar to newsgroups in concept, but they work quite differently in practice, and this leads to an entirely distinct atmosphere. As we have already seen, newsgroups require newsreading software, or a visit to a Website such as *Google Groups*. Mailing lists work by using e-mail. Instead of posting via *Google Groups* or *Free Agent* (for example), you send an e-mail with the text of your message to another e-mail account held on a server somewhere around the world. That server is responsible for sending your e-mail on to everyone else who subscribes to the mailing list. Your message then arrives in their e-mail box, and if they wish to reply, they can send you an e-mail directly, post back to the mailing list for everyone else to see, or do both.

Characteristics of mailing lists

As you can see from the preceding paragraph, the principle of mailing lists is the same as that of newsgroups – a group of people communicating with each other. However, as the system works using e-mail, there are a number of quite substantial differences in the way in which information professionals can make use of it.

Joining a mailing list is also slightly different from joining a newsgroup. You can join a newsgroup by simply selecting it from the list presented by *Free Agent* or *Google Groups*, as we have discussed, but to join a mailing list you need to send a message to an appropriate e-mail address requesting to join it. (I'll cover this process in more detail below.) Although this is not exactly a big hurdle, it does require a little extra effort, and as a result individuals who simply want to advertise their products, usually but not always related to some aspect of sexual activity, tend to ignore mailing lists. As a result, the traffic is reduced and the posts are more focused, although this does of course vary with individual groups and lists.

HINTS AND TIPS

A general rule of thumb is that you will find more serious and accurate information from a mailing list rather than from a newsgroup, although this is not always the case. Please remember that, as with newsgroups, much of what is posted is opinion, not fact.

Mailing lists always have an owner, usually the person who set it up. The owner plays an important role in defining the nature and atmosphere of the list by deciding what subjects should be discussed, whether certain types of post (announcements, for example) are permitted, and limiting discussion on a topic if it is felt that it has continued for too long. The owner may also decide if the list should be moderated or not. A moderated list means that each post has to be checked by the owner, and only if the post is approved as appropriate will it be passed on for all members to read it. This is another major difference from most newsgroups, which anyone can post to, saying whatever they wish. A moderated list will generally be kept much more on track, with a smaller number of daily postings. The slight danger of a moderated list is that the list owner is all-powerful, and may delete postings for any number of reasons. This could result in rather a bland series of posts, particularly in mailing lists established by commercial organizations for discussion of their products, since the moderator may decide to delete postings which are critical. However, members of a list in which this occurs generally realize quickly what's going on and unsubscribe. Finally, because moderation is time-consuming there may be a considerable delay between a post being sent and its being seen by the list members.

Locating mailing lists

Unfortunately, there is no single comprehensive list of mailing lists, so it might be necessary to do a little research in order to find lists that are of interest. However, there are some very good resources on the Web that can assist in this.

Topica

Perhaps the largest single listing can be found at Topica (formerly known as Liszt.com), at **http://www.topica.com,** which provides details on about 100,000 mailing lists. *Topica* arranges the mailing lists (or newsletters, as *Topica* refers to them) using a broad subject category approach, while offering a basic search facility. This is simple to use and very effective; it should be a matter of a few moments to locate appropriate lists. Information is also available on most of the lists, giving you the opportunity to check on the subject matter before joining it.

PAML

A second useful resource is *PAML*, or *Publicly Available Mailing Lists*, which is to be found at **http://paml.net/**. This is also a large list, with details of over 7363 lists available. To give you an indication of the breadth of coverage of the lists, I've included part of the page listing mailing lists alphabetically in Figure 12.6.

A full list of mailing lists that *PAML* is aware of can be obtained directly from **http://www.alastra.com/paml/ indexes.html**.

Other resources you may wish to try are *Tile.net* at **http://www.tile.net/**, *Meta-List* at **http://www.meta-list.net/** or the *Internet Mailing Lists Guides and Resources* at **http://www.ifla.org/l/training/listserv/lists.htm**, produced by the International Federation of Library Associations and Institutions. Finally, you may wish to explore some of

Fig. 12.6 *"PAML" alphabetical listing of mailing lists*

the mailing lists hosted by the major search engines, such as the *Yahoo! clubs* section at **http://clubs.yahoo.com/**.

National Academic Mailing List Service

The final resource is one called *JISCmail* based in the UK at **http://www.jiscmail.ac.uk**. This service is funded by JISC (Joint Information System Committee, **http://www.jisc.ac.uk**), and as a result the focus of the lists is centered on the UK (particularly, though not exclusively, subjects of interest to British academic staff and information professionals), although people from other countries are not excluded from joining *JISCmail* lists. In fact it has over 2000 lists with over 134,000 subscribers worldwide. Figure 12.7 illustrates the opening screen at *JISCmail*.

Appropriate lists can be found by looking through the alphabetical list. The service (which replaces *Mailbase*) is still in the early stages of development and as a result has limited search facilities, although this will be improved in the future. Once you have located a list which is of interest, you can check through the information that is available on it, such as the members and the number of postings per month, and you can search the archives of the list as well. This will give

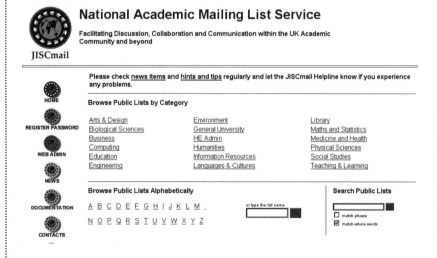

Fig. 12.7   The "JISCmail" home page
© JISCmail

you a better idea of the subject content and how busy the list is. The last point here is important: if you subscribe to too many busy lists you will spend all day reading e-mail and doing nothing else!

Joining, leaving and posting to mailing lists

All of the resources that I've mentioned so far will give you precise details on how to join, leave and post to a mailing list, and you should keep this information safe for future reference. I'll use as an example a mailing list called *Web4Lib*, which has been established for discussing the creation and management of library-based World Wide Web servers and clients. The commands used are specific to this mailing list, but the principle is the same, regardless of the list you join and wherever it might happen to be.

To subscribe to this list you send an e-mail to **listserve.sunsite.berkeley.edu** with the message:subscribe Web4Lib your name. To leave the list you send an e-mail to the same address with the message: unsubscribe Web4Lib.

These commands are sent directly to the computer that is responsible for administering the list, and it will be able to add you to the list or delete you from the list immediately. However, this e-mail address (**listserv@sunsite.berkeley.edu**) is not the address to which you send messages to be sent out to list members. The address for this is **web4Lib@sunsite.berkeley.edu.** It is important that you send messages to the correct e-mail address, because if you send a message to leave the list to **web4Lib@sunsite.berkeley.edu** it will automatically be distributed to everyone on the list and you will end up looking rather ignorant!

Some guidelines on posting to newsgroups and mailing lists

If you are an experienced subscriber to newsgroups or mailing lists you may wish to skip this section, since you will already have discovered by observation, or trial and error, most of the things that I mention.

Newsgroups and mailing lists can be a very useful way of obtaining information, and a few minutes research using

Google Groups or searching the archives of a mailing list may answer your question. On the other hand, you may wish to get more involved than just reading the newsgroups or mailing lists and decide to start posting, either to ask questions yourself or to try and answer those asked by others. The following are a few pointers that should hopefully make your introduction to newsgroups and mailing lists enjoyable and painless.

➤ Read the newsgroup/mailing list for at least a few days, and preferably a few weeks, before you start posting yourself. Each newsgroup is its own little community, complete with helpful and knowledgeable people, others who like nothing more than to pick an argument, and still more who enjoy causing problems. Take some time to learn who is who; that way you will quickly see whose posts are worth reading, and those posters that you can safely ignore.

➤ Read the FAQ before you start asking questions. Most newsgroups and mailing lists publish a FAQ, or Frequently Asked Questions, once every two weeks, or perhaps monthly. The FAQ, as the name implies, is a compilation of those questions that are asked frequently. To save people time having to answer the same questions over and over, the FAQ does this instead. It is quite likely that the question you want to ask has already been answered, and a quick check will confirm this; most importantly, it will stop you looking like an idiot!

➤ Do not advertise. Only a very small number of newsgroups or mailing lists allow overt advertising. If you post an advertisement to a group which does not want them, you will find your mailbox quickly filling up with messages from people who will tell you (sometimes politely, sometimes not) that advertisements are not wanted.

➤ Think about your post before you send it. It is very easy to write and send a post to a newsgroup in the heat of the moment, and if you post when you are angry you will doubtless say things you will regret later. If you are really angry, do not post a response until the next day when you have calmed down and can think rationally and objectively about what you want to say.

➤ Don't get involved in a "flamewar." This is a situation in which two or more people who hold different views start posting abusive comments to each other in the news-group. Flamewars are unhelpful, they do not add anything to a newsgroup and the only result is that you may get a reputation for being an offensive, childish poster, and people will ignore anything you have to say.

➤ Ensure that your posts are appropriate to the newsgroup. There is no point in sending a post about the latest HTML tag to **rec.pets.cats**, since the readers of the news-group will have no interest in the subject and will be unlikely to respond to your post in a positive manner.

➤ Resist the impulse to "spam" or cross-post your message. If you post a message to a number of different news-groups or mailing lists, people who take them will see multiple copies of your message, and if they reply their message will be copied widely in return, leading to a mess of postings across groups.

➤ When writing, choose a sensible subject heading that clearly describes the content of your post. Subscribers do not generally read every single post and use the headings of the posts to decide which ones to read. You are more likely to get a response if your heading says "Help needed installing Netscape version 6.x on Win 98" instead of just "Help."

➤ Don't quote an entire message when you reply. Keep your responses short and to the point, and only quote short sec-tions of the original posting that you are commenting on.

➤ If you ask a question in a newsgroup, try to answer one from someone else. This isn't a requirement, or even stan-dard practice, but it does help to make the newsgroup a use-ful, informative and pleasant place to spend time.

Summary

➤ Newsgroups and mailing lists are a valuable way of keeping up to date with what is happening in a particular subject area.

➤ They allow information professionals to keep in touch

with each other, to share and swap experiences, and to ask and answer questions.

➤ They can take up considerable amounts of time, and require thought and tact if your experiences there are to be positive ones.

URLs mentioned in this chapter

http://www.faq.org
http://www.faq.org/faqs/usenet/
http://groups.google.com/
http://www.yahoo.com/Computers_and_Internet/
    Software/Internet/Usenet
http://www.forteinc.com
http://www.topica.com
http://paml.net/
http://www.alastra.com/paml/indexes.html
http://www.tile.net/
http://www.meta-list.net/
http://www.ifla.org/l/training/listserv/lists.htm
http://clubs.yahoo.com/
http://www.jiscmail.ac.uk
http://www.jisc.ac.uk

Part 3

The future

13

The information mix and into the future

Introduction

I hope that you have found the previous chapters useful and informative, but I am aware that so far I have treated elements such as search engines and intelligent agents largely as discrete utilities. Of course, when searching the Internet on a daily basis this is an unrealistic way to approach the question "how do I find the best and most relevant information quickly?," since the best way of obtaining what you need is generally to use a combination of different resources.

In this chapter I attempt to merge all the different elements into a coherent whole, using some real examples of Internet searching. I also cover a number of other elements related to searching which I have included so far, and finally take a quick look into my crystal ball to highlight possible future technologies.

A quick glance through this chapter, with its many references to information professionals, might lead you to think that unless you have that sort of background it is not relevant to you. This is certainly not the case, and I'd like to emphasize that anyone may need to find the sort of information that I have referred to in my examples. Furthermore, you may not work in a library or use one each day, but you probably have a collection of books at home, and will find some of my points pertinent to the decisions you make about what to buy or how to arrange them.

Where do I go first?

You now have a large array of tools at your disposal which should make the task of searching the Internet rather easier. At this point, however, I suspect that you may be a little bewildered, since you have so much choice and so many starting points! You might well be thinking "Should I use a search engine, and if so, which one? How about an intelligent agent instead? Or should I ask in a newsgroup? Or on a mailing list?"

To begin with, let's go back to basics. If you are finding information for an end-user, the initial approach is no different from any other reference inquiry you receive, and if you are looking for information for yourself you will have to ask similar questions:

➤ Has the user clearly identified what information he/she wants?

➤ Are there any synonyms you should be aware of, particularly when searching global resources? – the term "football" means very different things depending on which side of the Atlantic you live.

➤ Does the user require a very specific piece of information, or an overview of a subject?

➤ Does the information have to be "official"? In other words, what level of authority does the user require?

➤ Does the information have to be current, and if so, current to today, last week or last month?

➤ What format does the user want? Text, a moving image, a picture, or perhaps a sound file?

➤ Does the information have to be in a particular language?

➤ Is the user prepared to pay for the information, or does it have to be free?

➤ Is the information needed once only, or is it part of an ongoing project, requiring frequent updates?

These are just a few of the questions that you need to be clear on before you can begin your search; I'm sure that you ask many of them at the moment, and probably some more besides. However, when using the Internet to answer queries you have many more resources available, and it is not difficult to work out from the list above which questions relate specifically to that, rather than to the more traditional searching which you have been doing in the past.

Once you have obtained answers to as many of these questions as possible, you are in a position to begin structuring your search. It seems an obvious point, but it is one which is nonetheless worth making – can you find the answer using another resource? It is very tempting always to think of the Internet, but an effective searcher requires the answer, and should not be over-concerned about the way the answer is obtained. If you can point the user towards a book, or the back-run of a journal, or pull a reference book off the shelf and obtain the answer that way, that is just as effective, if not more so, than logging onto the Internet, starting your browser, choosing a search engine, running the search, locating an appropriate site, waiting until it is displayed on the screen, scrolling down and eventually finding the particular fact required!

Some sample searches

Using an index search engine

However, for this purpose I will assume that you have already thought of using local resources, but have decided that using the Internet is the best way of searching for the required data. We'll take as our first example a situation in which you have to locate current developments in teaching children with dyslexia. A search for the term "dyslexia" in *Yahoo!* provides us with six categories for the disability:

Health >Diseases and Conditions

Business and Economy > Shopping and Services > Health > Diseases and Conditions

Regional > US States > Maryland > Cities > Baltimore > Health > Organizations

Regional > Countries > United Kingdom > Health > Diseases and Conditions

Regional > Countries > Canada > Health > Diseases and Conditions

Regional > Countries > United Kingdom > Business and

Economy > Shopping and Services > Health > Diseases and Conditions

and a total of 82 sites. The first site that I tried (a treatment center for dyslexia) was unavailable, but the second site, the Medical Dyslexia and ADD Treatment Center (**http://www.dyslexiaonline.com/center.html**), provided me with lots of information about the subject, including an introduction, a list of publications and information on medical treatment. The Center's page was updated a month prior to my visit and is maintained by someone who (according to the site) has published widely in the field. If I was in any doubt I could now visit *Amazon.com* just to check this, and obtain a list of the titles he has published. However, at this point I am satisfied with the authority of the site in question. The page provides me with a link back to the home page for the site, which among other things provides several video clips of medical diagnostic testing, identifying symptoms, discussions on the effectiveness of treatments, and several others. Of course, I am sure that I could have got similar information from a more traditional resource, but I am also sure it would have taken longer and would have had less impact.

Although I could stop my search at that point, I thought it was worth going back to *Yahoo!* to see what other sites they had available, and found several others, all providing me with appropriate information. I was also able to locate the Websites of several dyslexia associations and institutes. The whole search took no more than three or four minutes from launching my browser. Of course, if I had wanted more information I could have followed a variety of other avenues, but since I had the answer to my query I decided to stop at that point.

Finding a film quotation

Another inquiry, of a slightly different nature this time. Someone wanted to know if the well known phrase "play it again Sam" was an accurate quote. Rather than running a search on a general search engine, I happened to know of the existence of the Internet Movie Database at **http://www.imdb.com** which is a superb resource for film and film-related information. One of the search options provided is a word search, with a further option for searching the database collection of quotes. I simply typed in "play it again Sam" and was provided with 17 references which used a combination of these words, and I was quickly able to identify the correct quote from Rick Blaine to Sam in, of course, *Casablanca*. (Out of interest I went to *AltaVista* and ran a search on the phrase, to be faced with a total of over 8363 documents.)

I then decided that it might be a nice idea to see if I could obtain a sound file of the actual quote. An obvious place to look for this type of information would be a site which provides audio clips. The best way to locate such a site is to use a multi-search engine, and I chose to use Metaplus at **http://www.metaplus.com**. One of the results was a link to a site called the *Daily.WAV* at **http://www.dailywav. com/** (a .wav file is a type of audio file). This site provided me with access to ten audio quotes from the film, including the dialogue between Humphrey Bogart and Dooley Wilson. The site also pointed me to a large number of other links, including other movie sound file sites, four different newsgroups, other music-related sites, sound software, film and television companies and journals. Doubtless, if I'd not found the quote to listen to at the *Daily.WAV*, I would have been able to locate it at one of those sites.

DID YOU KNOW?

The last time I ran the "play it again Sam" search in AltaVista for the first edition of this book, I only retrieved just over 3000 documents. The total number of results has more than doubled in j ust two years.

Using mailing lists to find a speaker

A third example now, and this time I want to find someone who would be a good speaker on a course that I'm running on electronic copyright and legal issues related to the Internet. Since the course is running in the UK, they have to be geographically close. I decided to do a little lateral searching at this point. Good speakers often come from the world of academia, and are quite likely to post messages about the subjects they are interested in on mailing lists. On *JISCmail* at **http://www.jiscmail.ac.uk**, I was unable to search the archives since a full search function has not yet been implemented, but I was able to go to *JISCmail*'s predecessor, *Mailbase* at **http://www.mailbase.ac.uk** and search the archives for "electronic copyright." I retrieved a number of hits, several of which related to an online legal journal, and ten minutes of browsing gave me a list of half a dozen potential speakers. I then referred back to the mailing list to see what messages they were posting, took a look at some of their personal pages on the Web, and was able to narrow down my shortlist and e-mail my preferred choices to see if they were able to speak on my course.

Finding factual information using reference books

I'll take one last example now, lest I bore you to distraction. A friend wanted to know how many airports there were in the UK, for reasons best known only to himself. I started by searching in *AltaVista*, limiting my search using the domain:uk qualifier and the term "airports," but still came up with over 44,660 hits. I narrowed this down to 90 hits when I changed my search term to the phrase "number of airports," but unfortunately when I looked at them I found that there was information on Russia and Australia (remember that domain:uk merely limits to sites based in the UK, not about the content of those sites); although one site did link to two journals, I was still unable to find the information I required. I then decided to visit the British Government home page at **http://www.open.gov.uk** (this site will shortly be moving and by the time you read this I fully expect it to have moved to **http://www.ukonline.gov.uk**). A search through the site listed over 1000 documents that contained the words I was looking for. Deciding against that approach, I located the Department of the Environment, Transport and the Regions, and their home page pointed me towards their page on statistics, which in turn listed a number of individuals and contact points for civil servants who may have been able to answer my question. At this point I seriously thought of calling a halt, but remembered that another search that I'd done recently on events in London led me to the *Time Out* site at **http://www.timeout.co.uk**. Rather than taking a direct approach, I wondered what other sites like *Time Out* might contain the information I required, so instead of running searches on the subject I was interested in, I started to look for sites that might contain the information – a subtle but important distinction.

I remembered from my days of working in the library that

the CIA produced a useful world factbook, so it was only a matter of moments to locate it at **http://www.odci.gov/ cia/publications/factbook/**, virtually flip to the section on the UK and scroll down to the section on transportation, to find not only the number of airports (357), but also those with paved and unpaved runways of specific lengths! The only problem with the data was that it was based on 1999 figures, but that was good enough for my friend. (As an aside, I have to say that I think it's ironic that it was easier to find this piece of information about Britain from the CIA than it was to find in UK government Websites, though I suspect my American readers will not be surprised at all!)

There are any number of different ways in which the above queries could have been answered, but hopefully these examples demonstrate that in most cases the best way to answer a query is to adopt a flexible approach and not to rely wholly on any one resource. I could also have spent a lot longer on each of the queries, and I might have found more information, or alternatively I could have searched for another hour only to find nothing more. The longer you are able to devote to searching the Internet, the more confident you become, and the easier it is to know when to call a halt.

The examples should also demonstrate that in some cases the Internet will not give you a final result, but will merely assist you on the journey. This is particularly the case when you think it is going to be necessary to talk to a real live person. In both the transport and copyright examples, the Internet led to contacts, enabling me to talk directly to individuals if I wanted to. Indeed, I think one of the greatest strengths of the system is not just the amount of information it provides access to, or the currency of the information, but the way in which it can put you in touch with other people.

Incorporating the Internet into your overall information strategy

There are very few occasions when introducing the Internet will result in reduced subscriptions or the wholesale destruction of unnecessary materials. Let's look at a selection of resources to see how practical this is.

➤ **Newspapers**. All the large daily newspapers are now available on the Internet, and for most of them access is free, although some do charge for an archival service. Most newspapers do not, however, put their entire daily contents onto their Websites – although *USA Today* at **http://www.usatoday.com** puts most of each day's paper up on the Web, and there are only minor omissions such as articles that are not available for copyright reasons. If your information center only requires current copies of the papers, it is certainly worth checking to see if the subscriptions can be stopped, depending on the use which is made of them. Moreover, if you archive large back-runs of papers you may well find that it is worth disposing of them, since better search facilities can sometimes be provided by CD-ROM-based versions or by archival services from their Internet sites. This may turn out to be more expensive (certainly, if more news-papers start to charge for access to their archives), but it may be a faster and more effective way of providing a service, following the "just in time" rather than "just in case" model.

➤ **Encyclopedias**. The value of encyclopedias lies not only in the data, but also in the information held in photographs, charts and other graphical material. There are now several high-quality encyclopedias available on the Web, such as *Britannica* at **http://www.britannica.com** and the sixth edition of the *Columbia Encyclopedia* at **http://www. bartleby.com/65/**, and they are an effective and fast way of doing quick reference queries. This, combined with the power of hyperlinking to other documents, will, in many cases, tip the balance from a paper-based version to an electronic one.

➤ **Commercial databases**. As we saw in Chapter 9, many companies are now offering access via the Internet, rather than direct-dial access. Technically there is little difference between these two methods of access: both require software, telephone lines and modems. The crucial difference may lie in the different interfaces available, and generally the Web-based version will be easier and more straightforward for people to use. This can certainly be an incentive if you intend to allow your users to access such databases for themselves, although of course you might have to do some research to find out exactly how the billing structure differs. A small number of databases which have been made available commercially can also be searched free across the Internet, MEDLINE being one such example. However, although the data is the same as that contained in the commercial version, you may find that the Web interface is of inferior quality. CD-ROM versions could still prove to have value, particularly if the software provided allows users to interrogate both locally held resources and Internet-based resources at the same time. However, as with encyclopedias, if much of the information is held in a graphical format it may still be better to keep up a CD-ROM-based subscription for the time being.

➤ **Yellow and White Pages.** This is certainly one area in which I would suggest that the paper copy could be disposed of, though more so with the Yellow Pages than the White. *Internet Yellow Pages* allows much wider searches, based on company name, location and subject, with links to appropriate Websites, and the paper-based versions, as well as taking up a lot of space, simply cannot match the ease and speed of use. White Pages are a little more difficult, at least in the UK, since the body of information is carefully restricted. However, it may be worth doing some research for yourselves to discover if the online version is more comprehensive and current than the paper version. If that is the case you might discover you can save several feet of shelving.

➤ **Company annual reports**. It is becoming quite common for companies to put their entire annual reports on their Websites, making them searchable and adding hypertext links. However, it is unlikely that they will be doing the same with older versions, so it might be necessary to hold onto the archival versions, while managing quite happily without the current versions.

➤ **Dictionaries**. Dictionaries can be searched faster and more effectively online than in a paper format, and may also help suggest appropriate words (in the same way that word-processors do) if you mis-spell the word you are looking for. An online dictionary can finally overcome the age-old problem of trying to check the spelling of a word when you need to know what the spelling is before you can do it!

➤ **Specific reference tools**. This of course depends on exactly what the reference tool is, and whether there is an Internet version available. One of the first things that I did when I got access to the Internet in my home was to throw away all my film- and movie-related reference works, because I knew that I could get better service from the Internet Movie Database. For good measure I also threw away almanacs, a copy of the Bible and so on, simply because I knew that I could find the information I need more quickly and easily using the Internet than by trying to hunt through a printed reference work.

➤ **Official papers**. Governments are increasingly using the Internet to publish information such as papers, discussion documents, legal texts, press releases and so on. It is certainly worthwhile checking the Websites of your own government and ministries in that hope that material you might otherwise have to purchase has been made available free of charge.

Information professionals unite! You have nothing to lose but your books...

I am sure that many of you, reading the above bullet points, will be reacting with horror at the idea of throwing away parts of your collections. However, I think this is part of the fundamental change that we are experiencing in the field of information work at the moment. For years we have had to keep collections of books and journals in case they proved useful. As they were produced in a paper format, distribution of them was costly and took a long time. Even now, with the fast transport systems we have available, it is expensive to obtain a copy of a city newspaper if that city is 6000 or 12,000 miles away.

It was necessary to have stocks of information simply because it was so difficult to obtain. The Internet is quickly changing our perception of knowledge, in terms of its value and of its dissemination and storage. As long as I am able to obtain the information that I need within a couple of minutes by using the Internet, I have no need to store the same data on a bookshelf. Indeed, in many cases the information that is available electronically is going to be superior to the paper-based version. Not, of course, in terms of the facts themselves; the number of dead in the American Civil War does not change, however I get the information, but if I obtain it electronically I may be able to import those statistics into a spreadsheet and look at them in any number of different ways. Moreover, electronic contents pages and indexes can be searched more quickly and effectively than their paper counterparts. There will always probably be a need to have some information available in a printed format, and I don't dispute that. However, I firmly believe that we need to move to a situation in which we look at a paper-based product and ask whether we can get rid of it, rather than where to shelve it.

An understandable worry at this point is that if we get rid of all of the books and the paper, are we not also very successfully doing ourselves out of our jobs? If you have already incorporated electronic access to information in your information service, you will understand that this fear is quite unfounded. However, if you are considering embarking on this particular route, I'll go into some detail on how "less is more" in this instance.

...and an intranet to gain!

Intranets deserve an entire book to themselves, so it is not really possible to do them justice here. However, they form an important part of the jigsaw of the emerging information centre, so I'll briefly explain what an intranet is before going on to talk about how it can be used.

An intranet is an organization's internal version of the Internet. Information can be stored on a central server, or can be distributed on machines around the organization as required. Information can be made available in HTML format (the same as that used for creating Web pages), and links can be made to data contained in other formats, such as word-processed documents, spreadsheets or CD-ROM-based databases. Consequently, the intranet forms an entire "knowledge bank" for the organization. Information such as telephone lists, draft papers, discussion documents and so on can all be published on the intranet for people to access as

DID YOU KNOW?
Amazon.com listed over 300 different titles about intranets when I looked, and I am sure that will have doubled by now, so there are plenty to choose from!

and when necessary. If you're frowning at this point and saying "yes, but isn't that just a description of the existing network we already have?," I should also make the point that existing networks require users to access a wide variety of different tools in order to obtain the information which is required, while an intranet works by providing that access under the umbrella of the Web browser.

Furthermore, organizations such as Dataware at **http://www.dataware.com** are providing systems to further integrate information into a single cohesive whole. Hypertext links between information increasingly enhance a system in which data can be "mined," gathered from a variety of different sources and used to create new data sets. Of course, it is also possible to link to sites at other organizations, or to reach out to the rest of the Internet, creating an extranet.

The role of the information professional is central to the creation of a successful intranet; after all, we are talking about arranging and creating access to information, albeit in an electronic rather than a paper-based system. Who better to take on this role than those who spend their entire time doing just that in more traditional environments? The information professional is perfectly positioned to work with technical staff, the marketing department, public relations and so on to structure the information, choose and implement software solutions, train staff and publish information for themselves.

Far from having no work to do, a distributed system such as an intranet is going to mean a much more exciting life for the information professional of the future. There will be new technical skills to learn, such as HTML authoring, and a requirement to have a better understanding of how all these systems work. Perhaps more importantly than that, the professional is going to be drawn ever closer into a central key position in the organization; a "just in time" approach means that future information requirements are going to have to be anticipated, resources identified, organized and published on the company intranet. Intelligent agents will be brought into service to a greater extent, because it will be impossible to keep up to date with all the information being published, but even when it has been located, someone will need to check the data for accuracy and authority. The information professional will be able to

DID YOU KNOW?

HTML stands for Hyper Text Markup Language, and is the code used to tell a browser how to display a Web page on the screen.

interrogate the intranet to find out what subjects people are interested in, what topics are of growing importance and which are of decreasing value to the organization.

Commerce, the Internet and the information professional

In Chapter 9 I mentioned in passing the rise of commercial systems on the Internet, and how publishers are making use of it to increase their revenue streams. Methods of payment for the material that can be obtained are going to have an increasingly important effect on how we can all view and purchase material, and these will have considerable impact on future developments of both the Internet itself and the role of the information professional.

As we have seen, there are a variety of different commercial services available to the information professional and it should come as no surprise that there are a variety of methods of paying for the information required. The most obvious and widely used approach is to take out a subscription to a service in the same way that a CD-ROM subscription would be purchased – by contacting the company involved, ordering the service and paying the invoice. However, instead of receiving a series of discs you will be supplied with a user name and password. Other traditional methods of payment, by check or offline credit card transaction, are also widely used now and will be even more so in the future.

One payment method which I will go into a little detail over is that of micropayments. I have already alluded to this in Chapter 9 when talking about *Northern Light*, but I believe that it is going to become more common in the future. A micropayment system is a situation in which a company sells a product (very often an article) for a small sum of money, perhaps just a few pennies. While they do not make very much revenue from individual payments, the theory is that if enough people pay a small amount for a product the total revenue stream will be large.

The growth of commercial services on the Internet is having, and will continue to have, a profound effect on the way in which information professionals work. Before the rise of the Internet publishers sold information contained in discrete

HINTS AND TIPS

If you intend to use commercial services and intend paying by credit card, please make sure that you are using a secure system to transfer your credit-card details – the Website should state this up-front. If they do not, contact them before sending the information to confirm that your details will be encrypted so that no one else can read them. You may prefer to send your details by fax, phone or letter, but in the long run this may not be any safer! Do whatever you feel most comfortable doing.

units – books or journals – and a major part of the librarian's job was to provide easy access to this information by cataloging and classifying these units. Even after CD-ROM technology was introduced, and publishers began to distribute larger amounts of information, it was still done using a physical form (in this case the optical disc) to arrange and ultimately control access to the information. Although superficially things had changed, information was still made available in physical units such as optical discs, and this artificial boundary meant that users had to subscribe to specific databases of information based on atoms (the optical discs) rather than digits (the electronic information).

However, it soon became clear that databases could be pre-cached onto hard disk and publishers such as SilverPlatter ensured that their software could search across different databases. It was then only a short step to providing Internet access, as we have seen. It is now possible to allow users to access information in a completely different way; instead of having to choose individual databases to search, users can now ask for whatever information they require, regardless of artificial boundaries of database, book or journal. Online ordering direct to a user's mailbox has resulted in a situation in which the end-user can apparently bypass the information center entirely. Superficially, therefore, it provides an all-too-realistic scenario in which the organization can dispense with the services of their information professionals!

You will be pleased to read, however, that I believe that the role of the information professional in the new commercially aware world of digital technology is going to be more valued, rather than less. What the end-user is accessing (and in many cases buying) is what I refer to as "intermediate information," which only has value when it is used to produce an end result, such as a paper, a graph or a proposal. The value of this intermediate information will have been decided by the publisher or the author; they will have to make assumptions about who will want their information, how it can be used and how much the end result is going to be worth. A study of case law will be of particularly high value to a lawyer who needs the information in order to prepare a defense for a client, but the same information will have little or no value to a biologist, for example.

Information professionals are going to be increasingly valued for their ability in finding the right sort of information at the right price, or less if possible!

The role is one that should not hold any horrors, since in many ways that is what the professional is doing at the moment; the big difference is in the medium used. Users will need much more training, guidance and assistance to get the best value out of the huge amounts of information which will be available, and will need to use systems that have been designed and implemented by information professionals working with technical staff. Information professionals therefore become facilitators, helping the end-users obtain information, rather than the gatekeepers they have been in the past.

We will also see other changes in the information industry as a result of this commercialization. In the past, publishers have been able to create revenue as a result of their control over copyright and the physical methods of publishing and distributing information. In the future, authors will be able to publish for themselves and use micropayment methods to obtain financial rewards for their labors. The obvious result of this is that we will see a huge explosion in personal publishing, with little or no control. Information professionals are going to become increasingly involved with checking the authority of data, while the traditional publishers will need to encourage authors to continue to publish their work using them as the intermediary. Consequently they will have to provide value-added services in the way that BioMedNet is already doing (perhaps by drawing even more on the services of the information profession) and by adding that level of authority which will be missing from an individual's publishing efforts. This will inevitably lead to a rise in new electronic publishers, and information professionals are going to be hard pressed to keep up with this and will spend much time checking the validity of different resources. This is already happening, as we saw when we looked at virtual libraries in Chapter 10.

One final major change in approach is going to be the move from "just in case" to "just in time." Paper-based technologies meant that libraries had to keep large collections of information material just in case they were needed. Owing to the difficulties of transporting information in books and

DID YOU KNOW?
The Internet has created several millionaires, although none of them are information professionals as far as I know. If you want to find out who they are, visit **http://www.pulver.com/ million/**

journals, it was simply not possible to locate, order and obtain information quickly enough, so vast collections of books and other resources such as newspapers and more recently videos needed to be kept for the few times in which the information contained in them was required. Electronically available data, coupled with low fees for access, means that it becomes much more feasible to maintain the processes and methods of data collection (the terminals, the intranets and so on) rather than maintaining the data itself. In this new environment the emphasis shifts towards being able to find the required data quickly and effectively, and possess it for a short period of time so that it can be referred to, manipulated and then disposed of. Of course, some information will have an ongoing use within an organization, and the information professional will be charged with obtaining it and putting it into databases, where it can be retrieved on a regular basis using text retrieval or database management software in such a way that the end-user can access it easily.

Future developments

Seven years ago very few people were aware of the Internet; many of us still focused on optical technology as the best or most innovative way of making information available. Within little more than half a decade, the Internet has taken over, as more and more people use it, publish information on it and make their fortunes out of it. Every day new Websites are created, new applications are launched and people discover new uses for the Internet. Consequently, it is a very brave person who would attempt to predict what will happen in this fast-changing environment. Perhaps the only certainty is that change will continue at frightening speed and the map will be constantly changing. In the first edition of this book I looked at some of the advances that I was expecting with the Internet, and it's interesting to look back at what I predicted to see what exactly has happened.

➤ The rise of intelligent agents. At the moment these are in their infancy; if you have tried out some of those mentioned in Chapter 11 this will come as no surprise at all. However, they will continue to improve and the level of sophistication will increase. Within a short space of time I expect them to become the preferred method of locating information for everything except the "quick and dirty" search. Agents will be incorporated directly into intranets, and as they locate and retrieve information they will be able to import it directly into appropriate applications and will be able to alert staff to the existence of new data. The role of the information professional here will be to monitor the retrieved information and assess its value to the organization, to say nothing of being the individual who sets up the search profiles, updating them as necessary.

Intelligent agents have not yet taken off in the way that I was expecting, which is something that I've found disappointing. There are some good examples of intelligent agents, as we have already seen, but they are still something of a minority interest. I believe that this is because the vast majority of users tend to prefer "quick and dirty" methods for one-off searches. Information professionals who need to do more in-depth searching are using intelligent agents, but they are still making use of commercial databases for much of their ongoing work, obviating the need for an agent.

However, I am prepared to stick with this prediction because I do think that agents have a particular role to fulfill, but it will take rather longer before they are able to compete with traditional search engines.

➤ Search engines will need to compete with agents, but I suspect that they will do this by incorporating them into the services they provide. We can already see search engines such as *Yahoo!* providing personalized pages, and this trend will continue. The search engines will be able to monitor the searches that are being run, learn from the sites which are retrieved from the results returned, and run further searches automatically without prompting.

This prediction is coming true as more search engines are finding it necessary to offer added incentives for using their services in order to attract users to their systems. We will continue to see search engines adding to their range of services, although in the main I believe that this will be by adding more facilities such as chat rooms, free e-mail accounts and Web space, bulletin boards and so on. I doubt that the search technologies will, however, be substantially increased because the majority of people who use search engines are not sophisticated users (indeed why should they be?) and are happy with existing search facilities.

➤ Micropayments will begin to reshape the whole publishing industry. Authors will be in a position to publish their work directly onto the Web and will be able to charge users small amounts of money every time their articles are retrieved, and as I discussed in Chapter 9, systems are already being put in place to facilitate this. Publishers will need to offset this loss of revenue by providing added-value services, perhaps by following the BioMedNet example, and will need to create communities of interest, links to new services and resources, and so on. As now, they will be in a good position to allocate a level of authority to a publication by sending it for peer review. However, instead of this whole process taking months, faster communications will ensure that scientific and medical papers, for example, will be released much more quickly than at present.

Micropayments have not taken off in the way that I was expecting, and some services that I mentioned in the first edition of the book have failed to take off in popularity or indeed have ceased to exist. However, in other cases (such as "Northern Light") it is becoming increasingly easy to order full-text articles via the Internet, so I don't think that I was entirely incorrect here. Having said that, I'll revise my prediction somewhat: if a "killer application" is launched in the next few years to make it easier to create an Internet bank account which supports, and is supported by, a large number of merchants, micropayments may start to increase in popularity. However, I suspect that we're talking several years rather than months in this case.

➤ Another implication leading on from this is that the traditional approach to scholarly publishing will dramatically change. University presses will need to evolve rapidly as less is published in paper formats and more electronically. Staff will need to reskill in order to take advantage of more flexible methods of publishing. Articles will increasingly include a rich array of multimedia resources, but, perhaps more importantly than that, they will be constantly changing. Printing in traditional formats fixes an article at its publication date, but in the future I see no reason why articles should not become almost like discussions in their own right. The peer review process will allow an author to change, alter and add to a document, and then electronically republish it. Others will then be able to comment on it, and the author will once again be able to change the article in the light of this. The danger here is that no one will keep archives of "work in progress," so it will be necessary to establish systems that store earlier versions of a work in order to keep the historical perspective. Information professionals will, paradoxically, need to be as involved with the historical data as with the new.

Much work is already being done in this area and there are many debates currently going on, looking at the ways in which academic publications can be archived and made available. This is an area of flux, which I expect to continue for several years until authors and publishers can come to some sort of agreement on the ways in which articles can be made available.

➤ Online journals will proliferate. Since it is cheaper to publish electronically, and easier to obtain a much wider circulation, we will see a rise in very specific titles. Information professionals are going to have to spend considerable time discovering these new titles (either manually or by use of agents) and will have to check their authority before alerting colleagues to their existence. *This has certainly happened: there are many more journals available in an Internet form, or indeed only available via the Internet, than when I first wrote the above. I can only see this continuing apace.*

➤ Virtual libraries will become increasingly valuable as professionals work together to locate, check and publish useful sources of constantly changing information. It will not take long before they outstrip the search engines in terms of both usefulness and trust. A danger with search engines is that they mainly exist to generate revenue for their owners, and an obvious way of doing this will be to sell ranking positions, so that the company which pays the most will come at the top of a rankings list, regardless of how appropriate the content of its Website is to the search which is being run. Virtual libraries, run for entirely different reasons, will not be in this position, and can provide true relevance and ranking services.

One of the major problems holding back the evolution of virtual libraries is a lack of funding, so they still tend to remain quite small, certainly in comparison with search engines. However, as search engines continue to become increasingly larger (and therefore more unwieldy), virtual libraries will become more and more viable because they are able to locate appropriate information quickly without the problems that are associated with search engines. More virtual libraries are being developed, and if they can overcome another of their problems, which is lack of promotion, they will become increasingly popular as a way of finding information.

➤ Push technology will continue to evolve. Companies such as *Infogate* at **http://www.infogate.com/** are providing technology that will allow users of their services to keep constantly up to date with news by having it "pushed" to them as a data stream. Breaking news stories will be sent directly to the user's desktop, pager or cell phone. Live feeds can be placed on the user's desktop, or as screen savers, for example, and will alert them to information they have predefined, such as when a stock reaches a certain value, or if a storm is due to hit their town. Providers of push technology will increasingly work with a variety of information partners such as major news resources, so users will be able to define exactly what information they require, and when they require it. Such systems will therefore be able to provide high priority information that has been collected through the night as soon as the user arrives at work, while less important information such as the baseball or football scores can be delivered at lunchtime!

Push technology, as I predicted, is continuing to evolve. However, the main stumbling block to its widespread acceptance is the method of connecting to the Internet, given that most people still use a modem and a dial-up connection. Push technology works best when someone can be constantly connected to the Internet, so although it already works well in a commercial environment it will not really achieve its full potential until many more home users have instant access to the Internet 24 hours a day, seven days a week.

➤ Communication systems will also continue to improve. Mailing lists are very useful already, but they do not replace face-to-face contact. Video conferencing will become much easier, and groups of professionals will be able to meet on a more regular and convenient basis than is currently possible. Those individuals who still wish to speak directly to an information professional to explain their research topic and the type of information required will be able to do so, regardless of where they happen to be physically located. In a multinational organization research can continue 24 hours a day; if the information professional in London has to leave work at five o'clock he/she will be able to set up a video conference with a colleague in New York to pass on details of a search request and then go home, safe in the knowledge that the request is still being worked on. Next day a briefing might be waiting from a colleague in San Francisco who took the job on from New York. Rather than taking three days to obtain all the necessary information, it could be done apparently overnight.

Video conferencing is becoming more and more commonplace, and the proliferation of "Web cams" at home, where people can allow others to see them in real time, indicates just how popular this is becoming.

➤ If the concept of a 24-hour working day seems too horrific to contemplate, it will have benefits as well. Given powerful telecommunications, an increasing number of people will be able to work from home, and information workers will be close to the top of the queue. A multinational organization will be able to use its workforce more effectively, and if you decide to work an evening shift you can arrange with colleagues on another continent to take over their workload, enabling them to stop work early. As it will not be necessary to travel to work, people will be in a position to choose hours which suit them, rather than being dictated to by transport systems. *While the concepts discussed above are all technically possible, I think it's going to take a while before corporations really start to embrace the technology in a way that radically alters the workplace. We will continue to see more people working at home, but still connected to their work place via an Internet connection. This is a long-term change that will only happen slowly, but I'm still very confident that this prediction will come true.*

Summary

In this chapter I've opened up some new avenues for you to explore for yourself, and provided some food for thought. If you have gained anything at all, I hope that it is an appreciation of the variety of resources and possibilities which the Internet provides for the information professional. We will continue to hone and refine our skills, and although we may not be using information in a physical format in the future, the role of the information professional has a long and exciting future ahead of it.

URLs mentioned in this chapter

http://www.dyslexiaonline.com/center.html
http://www.imdb.com
http://www.metaplus.com
http://www.dailywav.com/
http://www.jiscmail.ac.uk
http://www.mailbase.ac.uk
http://www.open.gov.uk
http://www.ukonline.gov.uk
http://www.timeout.co.uk
http://www.odci.gov/cia/publications/factbook/
http://www.usatoday.com
http://www.britannica.com
http://www.bartleby.com/65/
http://www.amazon.com
http://www.dataware.com
http://www.pulver.com/million/
http://www.infogate.com/

14

Forty tips and hints for better and quicker searching

Introduction

Understanding how search engines work, and what intelligent agents and gateways are, is only one of the skills a good Internet searcher requires. There are a number of other important points to be aware of in order to ensure that the time you spend on the Internet is fast and effective. This chapter is a miscellany of the tips and tricks that I've picked up in the time I've spent using the Internet. Some of them may do nothing more than save you a few keystrokes, while others may save you a lot of time.

Getting online and moving around the Web

1 Get the fastest Internet connection you can. If you are using a dial-up account to access the Internet, a modem running at 14,400 baud is the slowest you can really use, and you can expect to spend a lot of time twiddling your thumbs waiting for pages to download or for your e-mails to arrive in your mailbox. Think of your modem as a doorway: if it's a large doorway, you can get people (or data) going backwards and forwards with no problem. If it's a small doorway, then people have to start forming orderly queues, and the whole thing slows down. Your modem is a little bit like that: the faster it is, the more data can go backwards and forwards. Consequently, it is worth investing in the fastest modem possible, and 56,000 baud will decrease the download time quite dramatically. A Web page which takes 50 seconds to down-

load using a 14,400 modem will only take 27 seconds at 28,000 baud, or 19 seconds at 56,000. If your organization can afford the cost of a leased line running at 128,000 baud, that same page will only take 6.8 seconds to appear on your screen. Of course, in actual practice you will need to consider that other factors, such as the time of day (mentioned in tip 2), will also affect the time it takes for the Web page to download onto your machine.

This is going to become increasingly important in the future as Web pages continue to evolve and include sound and moving image files as standard. You may already have noticed that some pages (usually those of corporates) are increasingly using multimedia, and without a fast connection you may just as well not bother to wait for the page to appear on your screen.

When and where it's best to search

DID YOU KNOW?

People use the Net and chat on the phone more in the run-up to a full moon than at any other time of the month. (http://www.theregister.co. uk/content/6/15501.html)

2   This depends very much on where the site is that you're interested in going to. If, like me, you spend a lot of time using American sites, you'll find it's best to search them either in the morning (up to about 12 o'clock) or later in the evening. This leaves the morning (their time) for the Americans to log on and get their news and mail, etc. It's surprising how much of a difference it makes! If you're one of my American readers, ignore this advice, and instead try UK sites during your afternoon, when we've all gone home for the day!

While the Internet doesn't really care about local/global issues, you may want to. Remember what the different time zones are: if you can get the same file or information from a site in the USA as from one in Australia, for example, my advice is to go to whichever country is currently "asleep," since you'll get a faster response rate.

3   Searching for sites in your own country? Try and do it at odd hours; if you're awake, it's a fair bet that most of the rest of the UK or the US is awake as well, and some of them will be trying to access the same sites as you. The more you can do first thing in the morning or late at night, the quicker it all will be.

Finding Web pages

4   The easiest way to find a Web page without using a search engine is to try and guess the URL of the site. It's certainly not an infallible method, but it is worth trying.

5   Become familiar with the major domain identifiers such as .com, .co.uk, .gov, ac.uk and country codes. Organizations will attempt to register memorable or easy-to-find addresses, so try a few possible combinations of name and domain identifiers. Naturally, if you do not find the correct site within a couple of attempts, you will have to fall back on the search engines, but the more you use the Web, the more likely you are to guess correctly.

6   Shorten the URL. We have all experienced this one – you find the perfect Web page with a search engine, and the summary looks perfect, but when you try to access it, it's not there any more. It may have been deleted, or it might just have been moved within the site. Shorten the URL one stage at a time and work your way back up the chain. Eventually you'll arrive at a page of some sort, which might give you an index to what else is on the site, and you might find the page you want listed at that point. For example, if the address you had was:

http://www.philb.com/search_engines/
publications/articles/freetext/altavista.htm
shorten it to:
http://www.philb.com/search_engines/
publications/articles/freetext/
then to:
http://www.philb.com/search_engines/
publications/articles/
and so on.

Finding information on a page

7   Once a page has loaded on the screen, you may have to spend some considerable time searching through it to find the keywords or phrases that you ran a search on, or you may simply wish to check a page to see if it contains the type of information that you are interested in. Don't

DID YOU KNOW?
According to a study by Cyveillance, the Internet is growing at an explosive rate of more than 7 million pages each day.

Fig. 14.1   *The Netscape Find box*

Fig. 14.2   *The Internet Explorer Find box*
    © 2001 Microsoft Corporation

scroll down through screen after screen: both Netscape and Internet Explorer have features that allow you to find the required data. In Netscape, either choose "Find in Page" from the Edit menu, or press Ctrl+F. This will bring up the dialog box shown in Figure 14.1. In Internet Explorer the command is the same and the dialog box is almost exactly the same, except for the option to match the whole word only (see Figure 14.2). Both browsers also allow you to search again for subsequent occurrences. One word of warning here: you must wait for the entire page to load before using the Find option.

8   Do not forget to make use of the "page up" and "page down" keys! It is surprising how often people neglect their use. Some badly written Web pages will also load wider than the screen, which means that it is necessary to use the horizontal scroll bar to see everything on the page.

Saving pages

9 Once you have viewed the page on your screen, you may wish to save it permanently. There are a number of possibilities here, depending on how you wish to save the data. The easiest method is to use "Save As" from the File menu. Figure 14.3 displays Netscape's pull-down File menu; Internet Explorer's File menu is virtually identical.

When you choose "Save As" (or Ctrl+S), you will be prompted to save the page as either a text or an HTML file. If you intend to incorporate data from the page into a word-processed document you should save it as a text file, because saving it as an HTML file will also save all the mark-up tags that were used to create the page. If you wish to retain the formatting, you can save as HTML, and then open the file in Word. However, if you wish to view the page offline using your browser, you must choose the HTML option. Please be aware that if you save a page in this way only the text will be saved, not the graphics.

10 To save the graphics you should right-click on each image and choose "Save Image As" (Netscape) or "Save

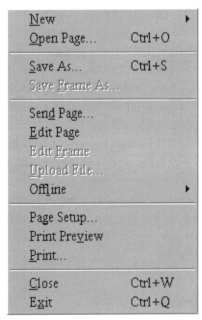

Fig. 14.3 *Netscape File menu options*
© 2001 Netscape

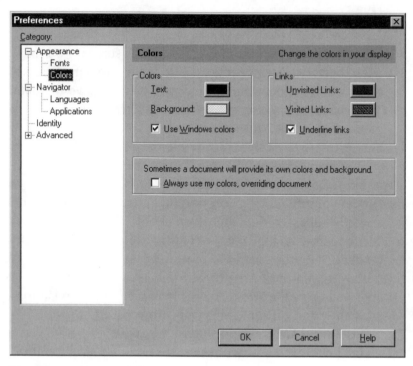

Fig. 14.4 *Netscape Color preferences*
© 2001 Netscape

Picture As" (Internet Explorer). That will display another dialog box prompting you to choose a file name and location. If you are intending to display the page using a browser, my advice is to save both page and graphic images in the same folder. You will then need to edit the HTML code on the page, so that the tags which point to the images are directing your browser to look locally for the images, rather than at a remote file server. It is outside the remit of this title to go into detail about HTML code, so if you have doubts about this you are advised to talk to a colleague who has responsibility for writing Web pages and can sort out the tags for you. Alternatively, in Chapter 15 you will find information about software packages which will save entire Web pages to disk for you, including graphics.

Printing pages

11 Alternatively, you may find it easier simply to print the

Web page that you require. It should print out much the same as it appears on the screen, though you may find one or two differences in formatting, particularly if the Web page scrolls off the right-hand side of the screen.

Sometimes you may print what appears to be an almost blank sheet of paper, which just shows the title and URL of the page. This usually happens when the Web page to be printed has light text on a dark background. The printer will not print a dark background (the waste of ink being astronomical!), but it will print the light colored text in white, giving effectively a blank sheet. If this happens to you, the remedy is simple. You need to override the page colors to insert your own. In Netscape, choosing Edit/Preferences/Colors will display the dialog box shown in Figure 14.4. Set the text and background colours to black and white respectively, reload the page and then print it. In Internet Explorer you can choose View/Internet/Options to use a similar dialog box.

12 Alternatively, you could simply highlight the text you require, and copy and paste it into a word-processed document, although you will lose the page formatting this way.

Displaying pages

13 This is an obvious tip, but turn "Automatically load images" off by using Edit/Preferences/Advanced in Netscape or Tools/Internet Options/Advanced/Multimedia in Internet Explorer. This ensures that graphics are not loaded. A good Web designer will ensure that alternative text is displayed in place of the graphic. If it isn't, you can try moving your cursor over the image and look in the bottom left-hand corner of the browser screen; you might see a new URL, which may give you some idea as to what will happen if you click on the graphic (presuming of course that it's a link, rather than a picture of the cat). If you decide that you do want to see the images, you can turn the "load images" option back on again, and reload the page.

Moving around the Web

14 If, like me, you get fed up with typing in the full address of a Web page, it will come as a nice surprise to find out that you don't always need to! In the Go to: box in Netscape, or Address box in Internet Explorer, you can generally get away without typing the **http://** and simply type in the rest of the URL as in: **www.philb.com**. You can, in some situations, reduce this even further – recent versions of the browsers will accept **.com** as the default, and will also make the assumption that the URL starts with "www", so you can actually reduce my URL to just **philb**.

Returning to recently visited pages

15 There are a number of ways that you can use to return to a page that you have recently visited. The most common is to use the Back button on the browser, which will take you back one page at a time in the sequence you viewed them. This is fine if you simply wish to retrace one or two steps, but is rather more annoying if you need to go back several.

16 Take a look at the location or Go to: box at the top of the Netscape and Internet Explorer browser screens, and particularly at the small down-arrow to the right-hand side. Click on it, and you'll be presented with a list of recently accessed sites, from which you can select the one you want to revisit. This is not limited to the current session. You can see this in operation in Figure 14.5.

17 You can also use a right-click on the current page; this brings up a pop-up menu which allows you to move backwards or forwards to other pages, which is quicker than moving up to the Back option, although you'll still

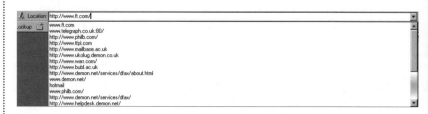

Fig. 14.5 *The Netscape option for showing recently visited sites*
© 2001 Netscape

Fig. 14.6   *Pop-up menu in Netscape enabling you to move around
the Web quicker*
© 2001 Netscape

be better off using the Go to: pull-down option if you
want to go back more than a few pages at once. You can
see this in Figure 14.6.

18 You can also see that this menu provides other functionality as well, allowing you to view information about the
page (View Source and View Info), add a bookmark, or
send the page to a colleague, as well as other functions
that are reasonably obvious.

Running more than one copy of the browser

19 Both Netscape and Internet Explorer provide you with
the option of opening up a second copy of the browser,
using Ctrl+N (for both browsers) or File/New/Window
(in Internet Explorer) or File/New Window (in
Netscape). This allows you to keep two or more Web
pages on the screen simultaneously, and is very useful in
a number of situations. Quite often a page will take some
time to download and display on the screen, and rather
than sitting and twiddling your thumbs, opening another
window allows you to begin to browse another page at the
same site or to connect to another site and download a
page from that as well. It may take slightly longer to
download both pages this way, since the modem can only
transmit a limited amount of data, but it can prove a fast
and effective way to work in some situations.

20 Keep an eye on the Back button on your browser, because
Web designers also make use of the "open new

window" function in the Web pages that they produce, and clicking on a link may sometimes open the target page in a new window while keeping the old one open. In my opinion this is poor practice, since you are being deprived of the chance to decide for yourself whether to do this; and, more importantly, it is quite difficult to spot that it has occurred, particularly if the browser is being viewed in full screen. It is usually only when you try to use the Back button that you discover this has happened, since the new browser window you are using has nowhere to go back to. This can cause unnecessary confusion, particularly for novice users.

Bookmarks

Using bookmarks

21 Both Netscape and Internet Explorer allow you to create bookmarks or favorites, which are really just shortcuts to frequently accessed pages. Once you have discovered a valuable page, it is always worth bookmarking it – it can be quite frustrating trying to find a specific page the second time around without re-running a search or hunting through pages trying to find that elusive link! Creating a bookmark or favorite is straightforward – simply click on the Bookmarks/Add Bookmark option in Netscape, or Favorites/Add to Favorites option in Internet Explorer, and the page will be added to the list.

22 When the browser adds the page to the list, it looks at the HTML title element on the page and uses that. If the title is sensible, such as "Phil Bradley's Home Page," you will probably remember exactly why the page was bookmarked, but if the title is something less informative, such as "My Home Page," it will be necessary either to go back to the page in order to jog your memory or to edit the title yourself to something more sensible. I'll cover just how that is done in a moment.

23 Give serious thought to deciding on the best way to arrange your bookmarks as early as possible, to limit the amount of sorting that has to be done in the future. Once you start adding Web pages to your bookmarks, before

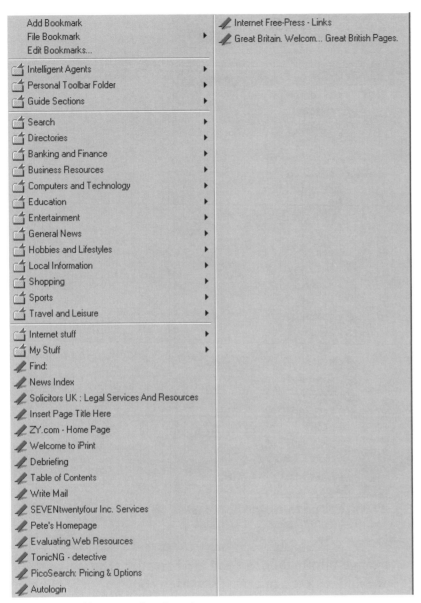

Fig. 14.7 *Netscape bookmarks*
© 2001 Netscape

long you will have created a list that covers several hundred sites, making the process of finding a specific page quite difficult. A sensible list of folders and subfolders will avoid the mess and confusion that results from a single list. Both Netscape and Internet Explorer provide options to arrange the bookmarks into a hierarchical structure very similar in principle to the method used by *Yahoo!* to

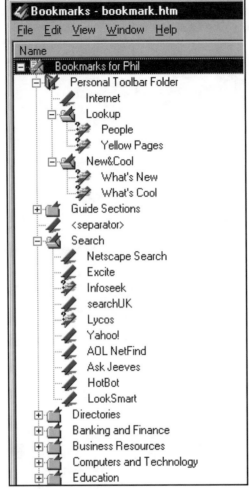

Fig. 14.8   *Editing Netscape bookmarks*
© 2001 Netscape

arrange information, so you are basically creating your own index to the Internet. Netscape comes with a number of bookmarks pre-set in categories, as can be seen in Figure 14.7 with some of my own.

Editing bookmarks

24 If you choose to add more bookmarks, by default they will simply appear in a chronological list at the end of the current listing. A more sensible way to use the power of bookmarking is to add a new bookmark and then use the Edit feature to move it either to a pre-existing folder or to a new

Intelligent Agents	▶	UMBC Agent Web
Personal Toolbar Folder	▶	The Daily Briefing
Guide Sections	▶	Shopping Explorer - T...t way to shop on-line
Search	▶	INTELLIGENT AGENTS GROUP (IAG) HOME PAGE
Directories	▶	CWSApps - 32-bit Internet Agents
Banking and Finance	▶	BullsEye Registration for Download
Business Resources	▶	FerretSoft
Computers and Technology	▶	The Phil Bradley Times

Fig. 14.9 *A new Netscape bookmarks folder – Intelligent Agents*
© 2001 Netscape

folder created from scratch. This will bring up a new dialog box that looks something like that seen in Figure 14.8.

Clicking on File/New Folder allows you to add a new folder to the bookmark list, and then it becomes a simple operation to click and drag bookmarked pages into the new folder. Figure 14.9 shows the same list as found in Figure 14.8, but with the addition of a new folder called Intelligent Agents. The name of any folder or bookmark title can be changed by going to the Edit menu, choosing Bookmark Properties, and entering a more suitable name for the item. Although I have chosen Netscape Navigator here, Internet Explorer has the same functionality within its Favorites menu. If you choose Favorites/Organize Favorites, Internet Explorer displays a dialog box similar to Figure 14.10, and you can then add, delete, move and rename shortcuts to personalize the list in the same way as can be done with Netscape.

Updating bookmarks

25 Netscape also has a very useful feature allowing you to update your bookmarks regularly. The View menu has an option Update Bookmarks, and if this is chosen, Netscape will visit each bookmarked page in turn to see if it has been updated since you last visited it. This is done quickly and effectively, and a little icon displayed next to each page that has changed. This of course means that it is not necessary to go and visit each page manually, since the browser will do this more quickly itself. Internet Explorer has its own, rather more complex, updating facility called Subscriptions.

DID YOU KNOW?
Over 10% of Internet links are broken.
**(http://news.bbc.co.
uk/hi/english/sci/tech/
newsid_790000/
790685.stm)**

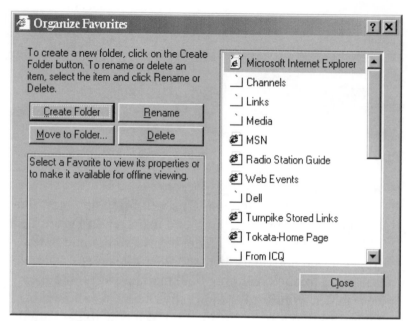

Fig. 14.10 *Organizing Favorites with Internet Explorer*
© 2001 Microsoft Corporation

26 Alternatively, there is a Web-based utility called URL-minder that keeps a track of the Web pages you are interested in and sends you an e-mail when they change. It's a perfect resource for monitoring URLs on your behalf. More information on URL-minder can be found at: **http://mindit.netmind.com/**.

Bookmarking searches

27 A final, and very powerful, feature of the bookmark facility is that it can be used to bookmark searches which have been run using a search engine such as *AltaVista*, for example. Run a search with your favorite search engine, and once it has returned a set of results, bookmark that page. What has actually been bookmarked for you is the search that has been run, and not the actual results being shown on the screen. When that bookmark is used in the future the search will be re-run, giving an updated list of Web pages. This can be helpful if used in conjunction with a date limit, since it means that it is easy to create a current awareness service.

Choose a new home page

28 When you install a browser, it will default to opening the home page of the company that created it. While there is useful information to be found at the homes of both Netscape and Microsoft, you will probably find in a short space of time that your first port of call is a search engine, or perhaps the home page of your own organization. Rather than bookmarking it, you can tell the browser that it should load that page as its home page. Both browsers that I use always start by loading *AltaVista*, for example, since I usually go onto the Web to look for something, and that is my preferred search engine.

To change the home page in Netscape choose Edit/ Preferences/Navigator/Home page, and in Internet Explorer choose Tools/Internet Options/General/Home page, and simply type in the new URL that you wish to make your home page. If you wish, you can also tell the browser to open your home page automatically at start up.

29 Alternatively, there is no reason why you should not create your own home page, writing HTML code to set links to useful pages, different search engines or virtual libraries, for example. Once you have done this, you can simply tell the browser to look locally on your hard disk to find the new home page, using the method just described. If you wish to do this, but are not confident in writing HTML pages yourself, you could copy the HTML code that I have included as Appendix 1, save the file onto your hard disk, and point your browser to that. It should look very much like the screenshot in Figure 14.11. A new home page, listing useful search engines, created in a matter of moments!

A more extensive version, including more search engines, can be found at my Website at **http://www. philb.com/** and you are welcome to copy and edit the page for your own needs.

Getting more out of your browser's cache

30 Understand your browser's cache. When your browser visits a page, it copies the information (both the text and

Search Engines Starter Page.

The search engines listed below will help you find what you are looking for on the Internet.

General Search Engines		Name of the Search Engine
	Free text search engines	Alta Vista
		HotBot
		Lycos
		Northernlight
	Index based search engines	Excite
		Metaplus
		Yahoo
	Multi-search engines	Internet Sleuth
		Inference find
Yellow and White pages		Biographies
		Electronic Yellow Pages
		FOUR11
		Who's Who Online
Searching for political/country information		CIA World Factbook
		EuroFerret
		European Maps
		British Government

Fig. 14.11 *A search engines home page*

the graphics) back onto your own computer and displays the page on the screen. It does this by storing the information in a cache, in memory or as temporary files on the hard disk. When you ask to view a page that you have recently looked at, the browser is intelligent enough to retrieve it from its cache, rather than going back to the original server and obtaining the information all over again. That is why you will generally find that pages you have recently visited will appear on your screen virtually instantaneously.

Both Netscape and Internet Explorer provide you with options to increase the size of your cache, which means that more pages can be stored; if the cache is small, the browsers are constantly overwriting old pages with new ones, increasing the chance that they will have to revisit sites. The larger the cache, the less this will happen.

In Netscape click on Edit/Preferences and then click on the "+" sign to the left of the Advanced options, and you should then see the dialog shown in Figure 14.12. This will then allow you to increase both the disk and the

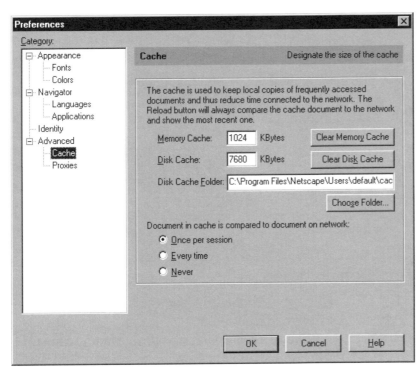

Fig. 14.12 *Configuring Netscape's cache*
© 2001 Netscape

Fig. 14.13 *Changing Internet Explorer's cache*
© 2001 Microsoft Corporation

memory cache. The sizes you can increase them to depend on the configuration of your computer, and the amount of hard disk space and memory it has available. If you have any doubts you should contact your technical support staff.

In Internet Explorer it is necessary to choose Tools/ Internet Options/General/Temporary Internet files/ Settings, at which point you should see a dialog box similar to that shown in Figure 14.13. Simply slide the bar across to the right; the further you move it, the more space will be assigned to the cache. Once again, if you are in any doubt, contact your technical support staff.

Productivity tips

31 Add favorite pages to the browser toolbar. Although the Favorites/Bookmark option is very useful, there may be times when you use a particular page so often it can still be a nuisance to have to click on the menu and find the page that you want. Both Netscape and Internet Explorer allow users to add particular pages to a toolbar below the Location/Address bar. You can see examples of both in Figures 14.14 and Figure 14.15.

This can be achieved very easily. In Netscape there is a small icon to the left of "Location." Simply visit the page you wish to add to your links, and then click and drag that icon down to the next line, and that link will then be added and will be permanently available. If you need to delete it, simply edit your bookmarks and remove it from the section entitled "Personal Toolbar Folder." In Internet Explorer click on the icon in the Address box, to the left of the URL for the Web page that you wish to add, click and drag into the links section, and once again that will remain until you delete it, which you can do by right-clicking your mouse over the link and choosing Delete.

32 Autocomplete. More recent versions of Internet Explorer (version 5.x upwards) provide you with the ability to autocomplete forms, URLs, password boxes and so on. To configure this go to Tools/Internet Options/Content/ AutoComplete and check or uncheck the appropriate boxes.

Fig. 14.14   *The Netscape toolbar links*
     © 2001 Netscape

Fig. 14.15   *The Internet Explorer toolbar links*
     © 2001 Microsoft Corporation

33 Changing font sizes. If you use a wheel mouse (that is to say a mouse that has a little wheel situated between the two mouse buttons) you can alter the text size on the screen by holding down the Control [Ctrl] key and move the wheel one way or another.

34 Moving around a page. If you have scrolled a long way down a page, Internet Explorer allows you to return quickly to the top of the page just by hitting the Home key on your keyboard.

35 Use keyboard shortcuts. If you prefer using a keyboard to your mouse, you may prefer to use some alternative key-strokes to pointing and clicking. All of the following will work with both versions of browsers:

[Ctrl] + [B] opens the Bookmarks or Favorites window.
[Ctrl] + [D] will add a new Bookmark or Favorite.
[Ctrl] + [F] is the same as Edit/Find.
[Ctrl] + [H] opens the History window.
[Ctrl] + [N] will open a new browser window.
[Alt] + left arrow will take you back one page.
[Alt] + right arrow will take you forward one page.
[Esc] is the same as clicking on the stop icon.

36 Viewing .pdf files. Sometimes an author does not wish to create an HTML version of a document; for various reasons it may be important for viewers to see the document in its original format, such as a government paper, for example. Consequently they will have uploaded a .pdf version of the file to their Webspace. In order to view these documents in their original format you should obtain a copy of Adobe Acrobat, which you can download for free at **http://www.adobe.com/products/ acrobat/readstep.html**. When you install this you

should find an option to tell it to locate your browser. In future when you click on a .pdf link the browser will download the file and then pass control over to Adobe Acrobat, allowing you to view the file in its original format.

37 Opening a previously saved Web page. If you have a Web page that you have previously saved, or if you are writing a page and want to view it with your browser, it is not necessary to go online to do this. In Netscape, simply choose File/Open page (or [Ctrl] + [O]) and browse through your hard disk until you find the page you want, then click on Open. In Internet Explorer the process is exactly the same.

38 Frames sites. If you are viewing a site that has frames, and for whatever reason you wish to open up the frame in a new window, simply ensure your cursor is in the frame you wish to open and right-click with your mouse. You will then be offered the opportunity for opening the frame in a new window.

39 Speeding up loading. If a Web page is taking a long time to download, rather than sit and twiddle your thumbs, click on Stop and then Refresh in Internet Explorer, or Reload in Netscape. The chances are that much of the page has already downloaded onto your computer, so Refresh/Reload kicks the browser into activity again and your page will finish loading much more quickly.

40 Printing hidden URLs. Not every Web author will type out the URL of a link – it is necessary to click on the link text to visit the new page. This isn't a problem if you are online, but if you print out the page the URL stays hidden. However, in Internet Explorer, if you click on Print, at the bottom of the dialogue screen is a box called Print Table of Links, and if you click on this and then print the page, all those hidden URLs are printed out at the end of the page.

Summary

➤ Even shortcuts which just save you a keystroke or two are worth using, because they will cumulatively save you a lot of time.

➤ Be flexible in your approach to searching, particularly the time of day that you search.

➤ Try guessing now and then – you never know, it may work!

➤ Learn your browser inside out. There are lots of little tricks that you can use that will improve its performance and effectiveness, which means that *your* performance and effectiveness will be improved.

URLs listed in this chapter

http://www.theregister.co.uk/content/6/15501.html
http://news.bbc.co.uk/hi/english/sci/tech/
      newsid_790000/790685.stm
http://mindit.netmind.com/
http://www.philb.com/
http://www.adobe.com/products/acrobat/readstep.html

15

Sources for further help and assistance

Introduction

One of the major characteristics of the Internet, as I'm sure you are aware, is that it is constantly changing and developing. It is therefore an extraordinarily difficult task to keep up with new search engines, changes in existing ones (*AltaVista* has changed its search engine interface twice while I have been writing this book), new versions of software, new packages, new sites, increased coverage for different subjects, new mailing lists and newsgroups, to mention just a few. Not only are the resources themselves proliferating quickly, but, as you can see, the list of things to keep a watch on is almost endless as well!

In this chapter I want to bring to your attention a variety of resources which can help you keep on top of what is happening within the world of the Internet; if you can spend just half an hour a week checking them, you should stay abreast of key changes and advances. Moreover, if you need to obtain a quick overview of a particular subject area, many of the resources that I mention provide useful briefings that cover the major points.

General information resources

Search Engine Watch

http://www.searchenginewatch.com
This site is maintained by Danny Sullivan, who is well known within the industry for providing current and practi-

DID YOU KNOW?
Isidore of Seville is the patron saint for computers, computer users, computer technicians, PC technicians and the Internet.
(http://www. catholic-forum.com/saints/ pst01058.htm)

cal information, and his site reflects this. *Search Engine Watch* is a resource that I use weekly, if not more often. It is divided into several sections:

➤ **Search engine submission tips.** This section is written primarily for Web authors and covers information on how to get a better ranking with search engines.

➤ **Web-searching tips**. How to do better and more effective searches.

➤ **Search engine listings**. Details on all the major search engines, meta/multi-search engines and children-safe services.

➤ **Reviews, ratings and tests**. Comparative reveiws, which are the most popular search engines, various tests and statistics.

➤ **Search engine resources**. A miscellany of useful information.

➤ **Search engine newsletter**. A free newsletter to keep you up to date.

Although the site is free, there is a subscription service available for $25 per year. Subscribers can obtain exclusive content which is not available on the free pages, more information than is contained in the free newsletters, in-depth fact files and access to research that Danny is working on.

Web Reference

http://Webreference.com/

As the name suggests, this site is a good resource that can be used to jump off into different aspects of the Internet. Some of the subjects covered are:

➤ **Design issues**. While the design of Websites might not at first glance be of much direct value to searchers, it is a good way of keeping up with new developments and software, and can provide pointers on what new packages you should consider obtaining.

➤ **E-commerce**. This section provides many links to discussion documents and sites that are involved in this growing area of importance.

> **Expert information** covering design issues, JavaScript, XML and graphics.
> **Reference information** on color codes, HTML characters and so on.
> **Services** such as scripts, validation tools, jobs and more.
> **Resources**. Links to information on search engines, new software, HTML coding, intranets and so on.

Trade Shows

http://events.internet.com
An impressive site listing and detailing major Internet-related shows, conferences and exhibitions.

The Internet Conference Calendar

http://www.conferences.calendar.com
If you want to find out which exhibitions, trade shows, symposia, workshops or seminars are coming to your city, this site and the preceding one are a useful resource to find out exactly that.

Browserwatch

http://browserwatch.internet.com/
This is another site which is worth bookmarking. It describes itself as the "leading site for information on browsers and plug-ins." The site provides information on the current state of play of the different browsers and how to get the best out of them, and gives a list of links to enable you to download the latest plug-in software.

Internet News

http://www.InternetNews.com/
Another useful site to keep yourself up to date with new developments in the industry. It has separate sections on:

> business news
> e-commerce news
> finance news
> intranet news

➤ Web developer news
➤ regional news
➤ recent headlines by topic
➤ career resources
➤ downloads.

CNET

http://www.cnet.com
Styled as "the sources for computers and technology," it covers hardware and software reviews, e-commerce, tech news, Web building, latest prices, finance and investment, downloads, and help and "how-to" tips.

ZDnet

http://www.zdnet.com/
This site provides more general information on computers and computing, but also has significant information specifically relating to the Internet. It contains new and breaking stories, articles on many different aspects of the Internet, statistical information and briefings.

The December List

http://www.december.com/cmc/info/
This site, maintained by John December, has a wealth of information regarding online communications and the Internet. It is a comprehensive collection for both trainers and students, providing access to organizations, forums, articles, and bibliographies.

Internet service providers

http://thelist.internet.com/

and

Access providers

http://www.thedirectory.org/
If you ever need to find out information on service providers, these sites link to over 10,000 of them.

DID YOU KNOW?
The Website **www.jesus .com** was created by a chap called Jesus as a personal advertisement for a female companion.

Internet hoaxes

http://HoaxBusters.ciac.org/

Never a week goes by when I am not informed by e-mail of some new virus which is going to destroy my computer. A virus warning should be taken seriously, of course, but the first place to check is this site, maintained by the US Department of Energy. The Computer Incident Advisory Capability (CIAC) monitors virus warnings and keeps a list of hoaxes. Please check out the warning first, before sending it on to colleagues.

The Netiquette Home Page

http://www.fau.edu/netiquette/netiquette.html

As I mentioned in Chapter 12, there are certain things that you should and should not do when posting to newsgroups and mailing lists. This site tells you everything that you need to know about how to be polite in your dealings with other people on the Internet.

Glossary of Internet terms

http://www.matisse.net/files/glossary.html

If you've ever wondered what some of those strange little TLAs (three-letter acronyms) mean, this is a good place to find out. This site will also provide you with information on four- and five-letter acronyms as well!

Mailing lists

As you'll have learned from Chapter 12, mailing lists can be a very useful way of keeping up to date with what is happening in various subject areas. I find out a lot of information about the Internet, search engines, new sites and so on simply because someone has been kind enough to post to an appropriate list with details, and I try to do the same in return.

I checked some of the resources that I mentioned in that chapter in order to find suitable mailing lists, and a list of some of them is included below.

JISCmail lists

http://www.jiscmail.ac.uk

➤ **lis-pub-libs**: This list covers issues arising from implementing the Internet in a public library.

➤ **lis-ukolug**: UKOLUG is a leading UK group for online, CD-ROM and Internet searchers, and contains lots of useful hints, tips and pointers to a variety of different resources.

➤ **pin**: Policing the Net. Issues covered in this mailing list focus on the ethical, moral and political responsibilities of the Internet.

➤ **sci-ed-inet**: Research into the use of the Internet for scientific education in the UK.

➤ **Web-research-uk**: This mailing list covers UK-specific issues and announcements dealing with Internet research on the Web.

These are just a small number of the mailing lists that specifically cover the Internet, and joining instructions and further details on all of the above lists can be obtained directly from *Mailbase*.

Topica

http://www.topica.com

➤ **net-happenings**: This is quite a busy list, since it provides information on new sites, events, publications and training, but it is worthwhile subscribing to.

➤ **tourbus**: This list provides a "virtual tour of cyberspace"; it is useful for novice users, and answers many of the questions that they have regarding the Internet.

Detailed instructions on joining the lists can be found at *Topica* itself.

Spam

I mentioned spam in passing in Chapter 12; if you recall, it is the Internet equivalent of junk mail. This is sometimes posted directly to newsgroups and mailing lists, but you may unfortunately also find it turning up in your e-mail box. If your e-mail address is on a Web page, if you post to newsgroups and visit Websites, or if your e-mail address is to be found in people servers, there is a strong probability that you will end up on various spammers' lists and will be sent unsolicited e-mail. I generally receive five or six such e-mails per day, offering me the chance to get rich quickly, make money selling products from my Website, launder money, have dubious conversations with scantily clad women, or various other illegal methods of making money. This last type is usually known as scamspam. I have heard of colleagues who get the same e-mails, up to 30 or 40 a day. Even if you do not read them, it still takes time to delete them from your mailbox, and to add insult to injury you are paying download charges for the privilege!

It is tempting to write back to these people, particularly those who offer to take you off their lists, but please be wary. Replying just indicates that the spammer has found a valid e-mail address, and you may simply end up on other lists, increasing the amount of unwanted mail that you receive. Many spammers will forge their e-mail addresses anyway, so you have no way of responding to them, or worse, you'll send an irate response to an innocent individual whose name has been misappropriated by these unscrupulous people.

There are a number of Websites that provide you with further information, assistance and detailed technical advice on how to combat this particular menace.

Help stop scam spammers

http://www.junkemail.org/scamspam/
This site provides background to spam: lawsuits, legislation, site listings, tips on spotting scams, and the opportunity to report any scams that are sent to you.

The Federal Trade Commission

http://www.ftc.gov
The *FTC* site is working for consumer protection, and provides legal advice and guidance as well as other detailed information on current scams.

SPAM-L FAQ

http://www.claws-and-paws.com/spam-l/
This document is the Frequently Asked Questions from the spam mailing list, which is a mailing list for the discussion of the subject, rather than a list used by spammers! As well as good introductory information, it goes into great detail on how to spot spammers, decipher e-mail message headers and report spam that you receive.

Fight spam on the Internet

http://spam.abuse.net/
This is a useful introductory guide to the subject, covering areas such as "What is spam?," "Why is it bad?," "What to do," "What not to do."

ZDnet articles

ZDnet writers have produced a series of articles on spam, and also provide technical details on how to set-up e-mail filters to reduce the amount that you get. You can obtain a list of articles by visiting **http://www.zdnet.com/** and running a search for "spam" and this will also provide you with a list of utilities you can download to eliminate much of it.

Using search engines

There are probably more resources that cover this particular subject area than any other, and I suspect that I could have written an entire book just listing and annotating them. I have gathered together a list of those which I have consistently found most useful myself.

Reviews of search engines collected by Sheila Webber

http://www.dis.strath.ac.uk/business/search.html
Sheila has created a very useful and constantly updated list of links to articles and sites that review search engines, provide descriptions of engines, and discuss search strategies.

Web search tool features

http://www.unn.ac.uk/central/isd/features.htm

Ian Winship maintains a regularly updated list of features and techniques for using the common search engines. It provides a useful short summary of what it is and is not possible to do with search engines, in a clear and easy to use format.

Search Engine Showdown

http://www.notess.com/search/

Greg Notess has established a site which provides summaries, reviews and descriptions of the major search engines, together with links to articles on search strategies, subject directories, multi-search engines, statistics and news.

The Spider's Apprentice

http://www.monash.com/spidap.html

Monash Information Services have put together a site which links the viewer to a great many different resources such as:

➤ a guide to useful search engines
➤ basic search engine FAQ
➤ planning a search strategy
➤ how search engines work
➤ in-depth analysis of search engines
➤ search engine ratings
➤ Web search wizard.

Web Search Engine Companion Chart

http://www.mlb.ilstv.edu/ressubj/subject/intrnt/
    srcheng.html

The Milner library at Illinois State University has created a chart that goes into great detail on many different aspects of search engines.

Phil Bradley's Website

http://www.philb.com

Modesty forbids me from saying too much about my own

site, but I do have a variety of resources available, for novice and advanced searchers on search engines of all types and reviews of a number of them.

What's new services

It is difficult keeping up to date with what is happening on the Internet: which new resources have gone online, new Websites, new mailing lists and so on. When people find new and useful resources they often post details in appropriate newsgroups or mailing lists, but a number of Websites also exist just to publish information of this nature. Inevitably, since the lists are usually chronological, focusing on new sites on a day-to-day basis, they are almost random collections, but they can prove to be a useful resource if there is a global event, for example. At the time of writing the World Cup is being played, with many new sites being made available every day, so the what's new services act almost like a current awareness service.

Internet Week

http://www.internetwk.com/
Internet Week is an electronic newspaper that provides information on today's news, trends, reviews, resources, awards, an events calendar, articles and highlights.

Yahoo! news

http://biz.yahoo.com/news/internet.html
Each day *Yahoo!* collects all the news stories (generally 30–40 per day) that they have found which relate to the Internet. This site tends to focus on the media and press releases rather than on new sites, and is therefore useful if you need to keep up with Internet business trends.

What's new from www.announce

**http://www.cs.rochester.edu/u/ferguson/
    announce.www/**
A useful newsgroup is **comp.info.systems.www.announce**,

DID YOU KNOW?
Terrestrial testing of inter-planetary Internet protocols is set for late 2001.
**(http://news.cnet.com/
news/0-1003-200-
6029873.html?tag=tp_pr)**

to which people can post details of new and updated sites and other related information. This Website acts as an archive of the newsgroup, with an index of articles for today, this week, this month and previous months.

The Scout report

http://wwwscout.cs.wisc.edu/scout/report
The Internet Scout Project comes from the Computer Sciences Department at the University of Wisconsin, and its weekly publication is of interest to researchers and educators, as it provides a fast, convenient way of staying informed about valuable resources on the Internet. *The Scout Report* can also be obtained via e-mail, and subscription details are available from the site.

Bibliographies and bookshops

If you are the type of reader who skims through a book, you will already have noticed that I have not included a bibliography or further reading list. There are several reasons for this: there are already far too many titles available to allow me to be comprehensive; any bibliography would be out of date before it was printed; and it is easier to obtain your own using Internet bookshops.

Internet bookshops exist in large numbers, and *Yahoo!* alone lists over 300 of them. I have listed below three of the ones that I use regularly, and it is only a few moments' work to produce a bibliography specific to your own particular needs.

Amazon

http://www.amazon.com
Amazon boasts that it has millions of titles available, and it is probably the best known of all the Internet bookshops. It provides customer reviews and author interviews and allows you to search by keyword or subject. The information returned for each title is basic, and the search features are limited, but on the other hand it is a very comprehensive service. *Amazon* also offers another service called *Eyes*, which is an automated

searcher, tracking every newly released book; it will send you an e-mail when a title is published that matches your interests. Not only does *Amazon* provide access to books, but it also has a comprehensive collection of CDs, videos, DVDs, toys, games and electronics.

Blackwell's Online Bookshop

http://bookshop.blackwell.com
This site allows you to search by author or title, and the results returned provide full bibliographical details, plus a description and contents list.

Online Book Search.com

http://www.onlinebooksearch.com
This site provides similar services to the other two, allowing you to search for author, title, ISBN, publisher or series. It also quickly compares prices at twenty stores.

Software

The Internet has always thrived on diversity and variety: there is never only one way of doing something, and usually there are several. This is certainly the case with software: if one organization produces a utility to perform a particular function it will not take long before three more do exactly the same thing.

In this section I look at some of the different types of utility that are available, together with why you might consider using them. This is not in any way a complete listing, but should simply be regarded as an overview of some of the available packages. I have not given prices, since these change quite quickly, and many of the products available are either freeware, which means that they can be used for as long as you wish without payment, or shareware, which means that they should be registered and paid for at the end of the trial period. Further details can be obtained from the company making the product available in each case.

Although there are many different software libraries available on the Internet, the only resource that I have ever needed to use is the *Tucows* site at **http://www.tucows.com.** It has over 5000 mirror sites around the world, which means that it should not be difficult to find a site close to your own location in order to speed up downloads. Currently there are over 30,000 programs available for download, and *Tucows* has a good "What's Moo" section, listing newly available software.

Browsers

The two major browsers are of course those produced by Netscape and Microsoft. The advantage of using either of these is that they are easily available (often from the free CD-ROM discs found on the covers of computer magazines) and Web authors write and design Websites that utilize their functionality to the full. However, they do have their disadvantages as well, in that both of them are large and will quite happily consume several megabytes of hard-disk space, even on a minimal installation. Although these two are generally the default choice for a Web browser, there are over a dozen other browsers that may be more appropriate or effective for you to use.

➤ Opera: **http://operasoftware.com**
Opera is a smaller browser than Netscape and Internet Explorer, almost fitting onto a single floppy disk. It is particularly valuable for people with visual impairments or mobility impairments. Opera includes an instant messaging client, a Web search function, a presentation tool, and an e-mail client. The only disadvantage of the product is that it is not free, although the price is cheap, in the region of $39.

➤ Surfin' Annette: **http://www.spycatcher.com**
This browser is useful if you are likely to have children searching the Internet, or if you decide to make your machines available for public access, but do not wish to run the risk of users looking at objectionable material. It utilizes various levels of protection, and can block access by site or by words contained on the Web page.

DID YOU KNOW?
The very first browser was in actual fact *The Reading Wheel*, by Agostina Ramelli in 1588. **(http://www.qbc. clic.net/~mephisto/bush/ bush.html)**

Bookmark utilities

As we have already seen in Chapter 14, the bookmarks that can be created using Netscape or Internet Explorer are very useful indeed, and if used correctly can become your own index to the Internet. If you upgrade to a new version of the same browser, it will be intelligent enough to use your existing bookmarks, but a problem can occur if you decide to switch between browsers. Luckily, however, there are a large number of utilities which can convert Netscape bookmarks into Internet Explorer favorites and vice versa. Others will even take your bookmarks and create an HTML page from them, which could then become your start page when searching the Internet.

➤ Bookmark Converter:
   http://www.magnusbrading.com/bmc/
   Simply converts bookmarks between different versions of Netscape and Internet Explorer.
➤ Bookmark Wizard: **http://www.moonsoftware.ee**
   This utility will create an HTML page of your bookmarks, as well as converting them between the two main browsers.

Offline browsers

An offline browser will allow you to specify a particular site that you want to browse, and it will then go online and "collect" the pages for you, download them to your hard disk, and log off. You can then view the site offline, thereby saving connect charges. Such a browser can be very useful if you need to spend a lot of time looking at a single large site, particularly if navigation around the site is not as clear as perhaps it should be.

➤ Leech: **http://www.aeria.com/products/index.htm**
   Leech is a high-speed offline browser that downloads Web content to your hard drive and can be viewed at a later time. As well as a free evaluation, the product can be purchased for around $25.
➤ WebStripper: **http://webstripper.com/**
   WebStripper quickly and effectively downloads a copy of

a Website or page to your hard disk for later offline viewing. It can also revisit a Website to download new or changed pages. If you are a business user it can be purchased for less than $40.

Cache viewers

As we have already seen, browsers will store recently visited pages in a cache. They can then be quickly retrieved by the browser and displayed on the screen; the browser does not need to go back to the Website to obtain the same data again. If you are offline and wish to view your cache, these utilities will re-create the pages for you quickly. Internet Explorer in offline mode will allow you to view pages for the "History" window, loading them from the cache if they are available. If they are no longer in the cache it will offer to go online and retrieve them. This is slightly different from an offline browser, in that a cache viewer can only display pages that you have visited, rather than pages you have told the offline browser to go and collect for you.

➤ UnMozify for Netscape
and
➤ UnMozify for Internet Explorer
http://www.evolve.co.uk/unmozify
These products, produced by the same company, allow you to retrieve pages in both the Netscape and Internet Explorer caches. An evaluation version is available and it can be purchased for under $30.

Multimedia applications

The Web might have been just text a very long time ago, but now it is a riot of still images, sound and moving images. Browsers are able to cope with some of these different media without a problem – they can all display images, for example. However, an increasing number of Websites are utilizing other forms of data that browsers cannot cope with themselves. Many utilities exist which can be called upon by the browser to display this data in the appropriate format. Once they have been downloaded, the installation usually includes a method of linking them to the browser you are using so that the process of displaying data held in different media formats is done automatically with no further work on your part.

A good Web page will inform you that you are about to view information in a multimedia format and will offer you the opportunity to go to an appropriate Website to download the necessary application, so you may prefer simply to wait until you have a need to do this. On the other hand, it may save you time if you can spend an afternoon downloading some of these utilities beforehand, rather than having to waste time installing the utility in order to view something which is urgently required.

➤ Real Player: **http://www.real.com**
   Real Player will automatically play sound files and display moving images on your screen, and can also be configured to connect to Internet radio stations to provide a live feed.
➤ Acrobat Reader: **http://www.adobe.com**
   Acrobat PDF files are sometimes created by organizations or individuals who want to retain the original "look and feel" of a paper document, rather than change it into a HTML file. In order to view a PDF file, it is necessary to install a plug-in utility which can read it and then display it in your browser window.
➤ QuickTime Player: **http://quicktime.apple.com/**
   QuickTime Player will play moving images (with soundtrack) from almost any movie format.

Anti-virus protection

Sensible users will always be alert to the danger of downloading a file containing a virus, but will not become so paranoid that they stop using the Internet completely. It is certainly possible to download a virus, usually embedded in another program or document file, but in my experience it is highly unlikely. The greatest friend of a virus is anonymity, and most viruses are passed from machine to machine by individuals using floppy disks to transfer files, without checking either the files or the floppy disk.

This is unlikely to happen on the Internet, because you are making a specific choice to copy a file, and will in all probability remember where you got it from. If it later transpires that the file contained a virus it should not be difficult to trace it back to the source. Furthermore, any reputable site will check regularly to ensure that their files do not contain a virus of any sort. In the years that I have been using the Internet I have only discovered one instance of a virus being maliciously transmitted; given the number of files available and number of people downloading them, this is a remarkably small figure!

It is possible to pass on a virus using e-mail attachments. For example, a Word document may contain a macro virus designed to harm your system. If you receive any such attachment from someone that you do not know, I would suggest that, before opening it, you write back to them and ask them who they are and why they have sent you the file. In fact, even if you do know the person who sent you the attachment they may have unwittingly distributed the virus to you; knowing your source is not necessarily a guarantee, so please do check!

It is also always sensible to backup your hard disk on a regular basis, depending on how valuable your information is. Suggestions range from once a day to once a week, but you should seek advice from your technical-support department on this point. It is also sensible to have effective virus protection software on your machine, and I have given four examples of good utilities below. However, once again you should talk to your technical-support department, since they may already have installed such software on machines within your organization.

➤ Norton AntiVirus
   http://www.symantec.co.uk/region/uk/product/ navbrochure/
   The Norton suite is one of the best-known packages, used by over 15 million people worldwide. The software provides comprehensive antivirus protection at every possible entrypoint and subscribers can also obtain monthly downloads of new information.

➤ Dr Solomon: **http://www.drsolomon.com**
Dr Solomon's provides a wide number of different virus
protection packages for work, groupware, servers, home
use and for use on the Macintosh. Subscribers can obtain
updates to their software directly over the Internet.

➤ McAfee ViruScan: **http://www.mcafee.com/**
This product is well known and powerful, including
background and on-demand scanning. Updates are available from the site to catch new virus programs that have
been created.

➤ ViruSafe95: **http://www.eliashim.com**
This product offers online protection when downloading
files from Web pages, allowing you to obtain files without the danger of downloading a virus with them.

➤ Housecall: **http://housecall.antivirus.com/**
This is a free Web-based utility that will check your
machine for viruses while you are online. Although the
service is free, it may be quite slow, leading to increased
telephone charges if you pay for Internet access.

Firewalls

Linked with but not the same as a virus is a Trojan. As the
name might suggest, this is a very specific type of virus
which, if you download it (or it gets sent to you in e-mail),
will pass information on your computer back to the person
who originated the virus. Your computer then acts as a
server, allowing that individual to browse through your computer, steal passwords, run programs and so on. A firewall
can help to reduce the possibility of this happening to you,
since it will block access to the Internet, only allowing access
to those programs that you select. None of them are perfect,
but they can help reduce the dangers inherent in Trojans.

ZoneAlarm at **http://www.zonelabs.com** is easy to install
and use, and offers a high level of security. Best of all, it's a
free product.

Organizations

Most, if not all, library and information science groups are
now heavily involved in the Internet, by providing publica-

tions and training courses or by funding research. It is always worth contacting your local organizations to see what work they are doing in this field. Some national and international organizations' Web pages are given below:

➤ The American Library Association: **http://www.ala.org**
➤ Aslib: **http://www.aslib.co.uk**
➤ The Canadian Library Association: **http://www.cla. amlibs.ca**
➤ International Federation of Library Associations and Institutions: **http://www.ifla.org**
➤ The Library Association: **http://www.la-hq.org.uk**
➤ TFPL: **http://www.tfpl.com**.

Magazines and journals

Many magazines related to the Internet are now published throughout the world, and these can provide very useful sources of information: new developments, new sites, "how to" articles, information on software and so on. *Yahoo!* provides a useful listing of them at **http://www.yahoo.com/ Computers_and_Internet/Internet/News_and_Media/ Magazines**.

Summary

In this chapter I have provided links to a number of resources which can assist you in further explorations of the Internet, as well as details of software that you can download and install to make your searching more effective. These Web pages are worth visiting and bookmarking, since they make the whole process of keeping up to date with developments so much easier.

URLs mentioned in this chapter

http://www.catholic-forum.com/saints/pst01058.htm
http://www.searchenginewatch.com
http://webreference.com/
http://events.internet.com
http://www.conferences.calendar.com/

http://browserwatch.internet.com
http://www.InternetNews.com/
http://www.cnet.com/
http://www.zdnet.com/
http://www.december.com/cmc/info/
http://thelist.internet.com/
http://www.thedirectory.org/
www.jesus.com
http://HoaxBusters.ciac.org/
http://www.fau.edu/netiquette/netiquette.html
http://www.matisse.net/files/glossary.html
http://www.jiscmail.ac.uk
http://www.topica.com
http://www.junkemail.org/scamspam/
http://www.ftc.gov
http://www.claws-and-paws.com/spam-l/
http://spam.abuse.net/
http://www.dis.strath.ac.uk/business/search.html
http://www.unn.ac.uk/central/isd/features.htm
http://www.notess.com/search/
http://www.monash.com/spidap.html
http://www.mlb.ilstu.edu/ressubj/subject/
    intrnet/srcheng.html
http://www.philb.com
http://news.cnet.com/news/
    0-1003-200-6029873.html?tag=tp_pr
http://www.internetwk.com/
http://biz.yahoo.com/news/internet.html
http://www.cs.rochester.edu/u/ferguson/
    announce.www/
http://wwwscout.cs.wisc.edu/scout/report
http://www.amazon.com
http://bookshop.blackwell.co.uk
http://www.onlinebooksearch.com
http://www.tucows.com
http://www.qbc. clic.net/_mephisto/bush/ bush.html
http://operasoftware.com
http://www.spycatcher.com
http://www.magnusbrading.com/bmc/
http://www.moonsoftware.ee
http://www.aeria.com/products/index.htm

http://webstripper.com/
http://www.evolve.co.uk/unmozify
http://www.real.com
http://www.adobe.com
http://quicktime.apple.com/
http://abcnews.go.com/sections/tech/DailyNews/
    virus000530.html
http://www.symantic.co.uk/region/uk/product/
    navbrochure/
http://www.drsolomon.com
http://www.mcafee.com/
http://www.eliashim.com
http://housecall.antivirus.com/
http://www.zonelabs.com
http://www.ala.org
http://www.aslib.co.uk
http://www.cla.amlibs.ca
http://www.ifla.org
http://www.la-hq.org.uk
http://www.tfpl.com
http://www.yahoo.com/Computers_and_Internet/
    Internet/News_and_Media/Magazines/

Appendices

Appendix 1 HTML for a search engines home page

In Chapter 14, tip number 29 was to create a new home page providing links to different search engines.

The following HTML code can be used to create such a page for you. Copy it exactly as it has been given, using a simple text editor or a Web authoring tool, and then save it to your local hard disk, giving it a name of your choice, followed by htm as the extension, such as start.htm. Of course, if you wish to choose different search engines, simply replace the URL in the tag <A HREF="...""> with the new URL and change the name accordingly. Then configure your browser as described in the tip, and you will have a new and hopefully more useful home page!

```
<HTML><HEAD><TITLE>Search Engines Starter Page.</TITLE></HEAD>
<BODY BGCOLOR="#FFFFFF" VLINK="#0000A0" LINK="0000FF">
<CENTER><H2>Search Engines Starter Page.</H2></CENTER>


<P>The search engines listed below will help you find what you
are looking for on the Internet.</P><HR>
<TABLE BORDER="1"><TR><TD COLSTART="1"><H2>General Search
Engines</H2></TD><TD


COLSTART="2"><H2>Name of the Search Engine</H2></TD></TR><TR><TD
ALIGN="RIGHT" ROWSPAN="4" COLSTART="1"><H3>Free text search
engines</H3></TD>


<TD COLSTART="2"><A HREF="http://www.altavista.com/">Alta
Vista</A></TD></TR><TR>
<TD COLSTART="2"><A
HREF="http://www.hotbot.com/">HotBot</A></TD></TR><TR>
```

```
<TD COLSTART="2"><A
HREF="http://www.lycos.com/">Lycos</A></TD></TR><TR>
<TD COLSTART="2"><A
HREF="http://www.northernlight.com/">Northernlight</A></TD></TR><
TR>
<TD ALIGN="RIGHT" ROWSPAN="3" COLSTART="1"><H3>Index based
search engines</H3></TD>
<TD COLSTART="2"><A
HREF="http://www.excite.com/">Excite</A></TD></TR><TR><TD
COLSTART="2"><A
HREF="http://www.metaplus.com/standard.html">Metaplus</A></TD></T
R>
<TR><TD COLSTART="2"><A
HREF="http://www.yahoo.com/">Yahoo</A></TD></TR><TR><TD

ALIGN="RIGHT" ROWSPAN="2" COLSTART="1"><H3>Multi-search
engines</H3></TD><TD

COLSTART="2"><A
HREF="http://www.ixquick.com/">Ixquick</A></TD></TR><TR><TD

COLSTART="2"><A HREF="http://www.inference.com/find">Inference
find</A></TD></TR><TR

><TD ROWSPAN="4" COLSTART="1"><H2>Yellow and White
pages</H2></TD><TD

COLSTART="2"><A
HREF="http://www.biography.com/find/find.html">Biographies</A></T
D></TR>
<TR><TD COLSTART="2"><A HREF="http://www.yell.co.uk/">Electronic
Yellow Pages</A></TD></TR>
<TR><TD COLSTART="2"><A
HREF="http://www.Four11.com/">FOUR11</A></TD></TR><TR><TD

COLSTART="2"><A HREF="http://www.whoswho-
online.com/search.html">Who's Who
Online</A></TD></TR><TR><TD ROWSPAN="3"
COLSTART="1"><H2>Searching for
political/country information</H2></TD><TD COLSTART="2"><A
```

```
HREF="http://www.research.att.com/cgi-wald/dbaccess/411">CIA
World Factbook</A></TD></TR>
<TR><TD COLSTART="2"><A
HREF="http://www.muscat.co.uk/">EuroFerret</A></TD></TR><TR

><TD COLSTART="2"><A HREF="http://www.tue.nl/europe/">European
Maps</A></TD></TR><TR

><TD ROWSPAN="7" COLSTART="1"><H2>UK specific
resources</H2></TD><TD

COLSTART="2"><A HREF="http://www.open.gov.uk/">British
Government</A></TD></TR><TR

><TD COLSTART="2"><A HREF="http://www.excite.co.uk/">Excite
UK</A></TD></TR><TR><TD

COLSTART="2"><A HREF="http://www.emap.com/id/uk/">Internet
Directory UK</A></TD></TR>
<TR><TD COLSTART="2"><A
HREF="http://www.cybersearch.co.uk/">UKCybersearch</A></TD></TR>
<TR><TD COLSTART="2"><A
HREF="http://www.ukindex.co.uk/uksearch.html">UK
Index</A></TD></TR><TR><TD COLSTART="2"><A
HREF="http://uksearch.com/">UKSearch</A></TD></TR>
<TR><TD COLSTART="2"><A HREF="http://www.yahoo.co.uk/">Yahoo
UK</A></TD></TR><TR>
<TD ROWSPAN="3" COLSTART="1"><H2>Searching newsgroups/mail
lists</H2></TD><TD

COLSTART="2"><A HREF="http://www.dejanews.com/">Deja
News</A></TD></TR><TR><TD

COLSTART="2"><A
HREF="http://www.liszt.com/">Liszt</A></TD></TR><TR><TD

COLSTART="2"><A
HREF="http://www.mailbase.ac.uk/">Mailbase</A></TD></TR><TR><TD

ROWSPAN="8" COLSTART="1"><H2>Searching specific
resources</H2></TD><TD
```

```
COLSTART="2"><A HREF="http://www.ucc.ie/cgi-
bin/acronym">Acronyms</A></TD></TR><TR
><TD COLSTART="2"><A HREF="http://www.gospelcom.net/bible">The
Bible</A></TD></TR>
<TR><TD COLSTART="2"><A
HREF="http://c.gp.cs.cmu.edu:5103/prog/Webster">Dictionary
(Websters)</A></TD></TR><TR><TD COLSTART="2"><A


HREF="http://www.edoc.com/ejournal/">Electronic
Journals</A></TD></TR><TR><TD


COLSTART="2"><A
HREF="http://www.mediauk.com/directory/search.html">MediaUK
(Newspapers/magazines)</A></TD></TR><TR><TD COLSTART="2"><A


HREF="http://lcWeb.loc.gov/harvest/">Library of
Congress</A></TD></TR><TR><TD


COLSTART="2"><A
HREF="http://www.columbia.edu/acis/bartleby/bartlett/">Quotations
</A></TD></TR>
<TR><TD COLSTART="2"><A
HREF="http://www.ipl.org/ref/Search.html">Ready
reference collection</A></TD></TR><TR><TD ROWSPAN="2" COL-
START="1"><H2>Searching
for images/music</H2></TD><TD COLSTART="2"><A
HREF="http://www.lyrics.ch/">Lyrics</A></TD></TR>
<TR><TD COLSTART="2"><A
HREF="http://www.cs.indiana.edu/picons/search.html">Picons
(icons/images)</A></TD></TR><TR><TD ROWSPAN="3"
COLSTART="1"><H2>Searching
for software</H2></TD><TD COLSTART="2"><A
HREF="http://www.shareware.com/">Shareware.com</A></TD></TR>
<TR><TD COLSTART="2"><A
HREF="http://www.filez.com/">Filez.com</A></TD></TR><TR><TD


COLSTART="2"><A
HREF="http://www.download.com/">Download.com</A></TD></TR></TABLE
>
<HR></BODY></HTML>
```

Appendix 2 Country codes

AD	Andorra
AE	United Arab Emirates
AF	Afghanistan
AG	Antigua and Barbuda
AI	Anguilla
AL	Albania
AM	Armenia
AN	Netherlands Antilles
AO	Angola
AQ	Antarctica
AR	Argentina
AS	American Samoa
AT	Austria
AU	Australia
AW	Aruba
AZ	Azerbaijan
BA	Bosnia and Herzegovina
BB	Barbados
BD	Bangladesh
BE	Belgium
BF	Burkina Faso
BG	Bulgaria
BH	Bahrain
BI	Burundi
BJ	Benin
BM	Bermuda
BN	Brunei Darussalam
BO	Bolivia
BR	Brazil

BS   Bahamas
BT   Bhutan
BV   Bouvet Island
BW   Botswana
BY   Belarus
BZ   Belize

CA Canada
CC   Cocos (Keeling) Islands
CF   Central African Republic
CG   Congo
CH   Switzerland
CI   Côte D'Ivoire (Ivory Coast)
CK   Cook Islands
CL   Chile
CM   Cameroon
CN   China
CO   Colombia
CR   Costa Rica
CS   Czechoslovakia (former)
CU   Cuba
CV   Cape Verde
CX   Christmas Island
CY   Cyprus
CZ   Czech Republic

DE   Germany
DJ   Djibouti
DK   Denmark
DM   Dominica
DO   Dominican Republic
DZ   Algeria

EC   Ecuador
EE   Estonia
EG   Egypt
EH   Western Sahara
ER   Eritrea
ES   Spain
ET   Ethiopia

FI   Finland
FJ   Fiji
FK   Falkland Islands (Malvinas)
FM   Micronesia
FO   Faroe Islands
FR   France
FX   France, Metropolitan

GAGabon
GB   Great Britain (UK)
GD   Grenada
GE   Georgia
GF   French Guiana
GH   Ghana
GI   Gibraltar
GL   Greenland
GM   Gambia
GN   Guinea
GP   Guadeloupe
GQ   Equatorial Guinea
GR   Greece
GS   South Georgia and South Sandwich Islands
GT   Guatemala
GU   Guam
GW   Guinea-Bissau
GY   Guyana

HKHong Kong
HM   Heard and McDonald Islands
HN   Honduras
HR   Croatia (Hrvatska)
HT   Haiti
HU   Hungary

ID   Indonesia
IE   Ireland
IL   Israel
IN   India
IO   British Indian Ocean Territory
IQ   Iraq
IR   Iran

DID YOU KNOW?
The first African country to be wired into the Internet was Ghana.

IS	Iceland
IT	Italy
JM	Jamaica
JO	Jordan
JP	Japan
KE	Kenya
KG	Kyrgyzstan
KH	Cambodia
KI	Kiribati
KM	Comoros
KN	Saint Kitts and Nevis
KP	Korea (North)
KR	Korea (South)
KW	Kuwait
KY	Cayman Islands
KZ	Kazakhstan
LA	Laos
LB	Lebanon
LC	Saint Lucia
LI	Liechtenstein
LK	Sri Lanka
LR	Liberia
LS	Lesotho
LT	Lithuania
LU	Luxembourg
LV	Latvia
LY	Libya
MA	Morocco
MC	Monaco
MD	Moldova
MG	Madagascar
MH	Marshall Islands
MK	Macedonia
ML	Mali
MM	Myanmar
MN	Mongolia
MO	Macau

MP	Northern Mariana Islands
MQ	Martinique
MR	Mauritania
MS	Montserrat
MT	Malta
MU	Mauritius
MV	Maldives
MW	Malawi
MX	Mexico
MY	Malaysia
MZ	Mozambique
NA	Namibia
NC	New Caledonia
NE	Niger
NF	Norfolk Island
NG	Nigeria
NI	Nicaragua
NL	Netherlands
NO	Norway
NP	Nepal
NR	Nauru
NT	Neutral Zone
NU	Niue
NZ	New Zealand (Aotearoa)
OM	Oman
PA	Panama
PE	Peru
PF	French Polynesia
PG	Papua New Guinea
PH	Philippines
PK	Pakistan
PL	Poland
PM	Saint-Pierre and Miquelon
PN	Pitcairn
PR	Puerto Rico
PT	Portugal
PW	Palau
PY	Paraguay

QAQatar

RE	Réunion
RO	Romania
RU	Russian Federation
RW	Rwanda
SA	Saudi Arabia
SB	Solomon Islands
SC	Seychelles
SD	Sudan
SE	Sweden
SG	Singapore
SH	Saint Helena
SI	Slovenia
SJ	Svalbard and Jan Mayen Islands
SK	Slovak Republic
SL	Sierra Leone
SM	San Marino
SN	Senegal
SO	Somalia
SR	Suriname
ST	São Tomé and Príncipe
SU	USSR (former)
SV	El Salvador
SY	Syria
SZ	Swaziland
TC	Turks and Caicos Islands
TD	Chad
TF	French Southern Territories
TG	Togo
TH	Thailand
TJ	Tajikistan
TK	Tokelau
TM	Turkmenistan
TN	Tunisia
TO	Tonga
TP	East Timor
TR	Turkey
TT	Trinidad and Tobago

TV   Tuvalu
TW   Taiwan
TZ   Tanzania

UA Ukraine
UG   Uganda
UK   United Kingdom
UM   US Minor Outlying Islands
US   United States
UY   Uruguay
UZ   Uzbekistan

VA   Vatican City State (Holy See)
VC   Saint Vincent and the Grenadines
VE   Venezuela
VG   Virgin Islands (British)
VI   Virgin Islands (US)
VN   Viet Nam
VU   Vanuatu

WF   Wallis and Futuna Islands
WS   Samoa

YE   Yemen
YT   Mayotte
YU   Yugoslavia

ZA   South Africa
ZM   Zambia
ZR   Zaire
ZW   Zimbabwe

COM   US commercial
EDU   US educational
GOV   US government
INT   international
MIL   US military
NET   network
ORG   non-profit organization
ARPA   old style Arpanet
NATO   NATO field

Appendix 3 URLs mentioned in the book

Chapter 1 An introduction to the Internet

http://www.yahoo.com/Computers_and_Internet/
    Internet/History/
http://www.matisse.net/files/glossary.html
http://www.w3c.org
http://www.anamorph.com/docs/stats/stats.html

Chapter 2 An introduction to search engines

http://www.quoteland.com/index.html
http://www.allonesearch.com
http://www.ixquick.com
http://www.altavista.com
http://www.yahoo.com
http://www.aj.com
http://www.ask.co.uk
http://www.searchenginewatch.com
http://www.amazon.com

Chapter 3 Free-text search engines

http://www.altavista.com
http://www.philb.com
http://www.libraryland.org
http://web.realnames.com/
http://uk.altavista.com
http://www.lycos.com
http://www.hotbot.com

http://search.aol.com
http://www.espotting.com
http://www.euroseek.com
http://www.google.com
http://www.looksmart.com
http://www.searcheurope.com
http://www.webcrawler.com
http://www.northernlight.com

Chapter 4 Index-based search engines

http://www.yahoo.com
http://www.yahoo.co.uk
http://www.mckinley.com
http://www.net-find.com
http://www.god.co.uk
http://www.excite.com
http://galaxy.tradewave.com
http://www.nosearch.com

Chapter 5 Multi-search engines

http://www.thebighub.com
http://www.metaplus.com
http://www.metaspy.com
http://www.iTools.com/find-it/
http://www.dogpile.com/
http://www.ixquick.com

Chapter 6 Natural-language search engines

http://www.aj.com
http://www.ask.co.uk/
http://www.albert.com/demo.php

Chapter 7 Finding images, sounds and multimedia information

http://gallery.yahoo.com/
http://www.1stopstock.com/

http://www.ncrtec.org/picture.htm
http://sunsite.berkeley.edu/ImageFinder/
http://disney.ctr.columbia.edu/Webseek/
http://www.homepages.demon.co.uk/
http://www.aphids.com/susan/imres/
http://search.altavista.com/sites/search/topic
http://www.dailywav.com/
http://www.moviesounds.com/
http://www.soundamerica.com/
http://www.napster.com/
http://gwis2.circ.gwu.edu/_gprice/speech.htm
http://mmsound.about.com/compute/mmsound/
    mbody.htm
http://www.Singingfish.com/
http://search.digitide.de/
http://www.tucows.com/

Chapter 8 Finding people

http://www.altavista.com
http://www.hotbot.com
http://www.lycos.co.uk
http://www.northernlight.com
http://people.yahoo.com/
http://www.i-ring.com/find/find.cgi
http://www.bigfoot.com/
http://www.infospace.com/_1_4PW9TN503NB3D9I
    _info/redirs_all.htm?pgtarg=pplea
http://www.whowhere.lycos.com/
http://www.iaf.net/noframes-default.htm
http://worldpages.altavista.com/whitepages/
http://www.whowhere.lycos.com/Phone
http://wp.superpages.com/people.phtml?SRC=excite
http://www.bt.com/directory-enquiries/dq_home.jsp.
http://www.192.com
http://www.infospaceuk.com
http://www.lookupUK.com
http://www.friendsreunited.co.uk
http://www.classmates.com/
http://www.familysearch.org
http://www.jiscmail.ac.uk/

Chapter 9 Other available database resources

http://www.wkap.nl/
http://www.smlawpub.co.uk/
http://www.chadwyck.co.uk
http://www.bmn.com
http://chemweb.com.
http://www.silverplatter.com
http://www.forrester.com
http://www.ovid.com
http://www.ala.org
http://www.hw.ac.uk/libWWW/irn/irn.html
http://www.sfgate.com
http://www.telegraph.co.uk
http://www.amazon.com
http://www.amazon.co.uk
http://www.hammond.co.uk
http://www.northernlight.com/

Chapter 10 Virtual libraries and gateways

http://www.philb.com
http://www.amex.com
http://www.aa.com
http://www.easyspace.com
http://www.vlib.org
http://vlib.org.uk
http://www.ukoln.ac.uk/services/elib/
http://www.jisc.ac.uk
http://www.ilrt.bris.ac.uk/roads/who/
http://www.agnic.org/
http://www.animalomnibus.com/
http://www.ericir.syr.edu/
http://www.economy.com/dismal/
http://www.eserver.org/
http://www.contemplator.com/
http://www.lib.uiowa.edu/hardin/md/
http://www.hippias.evansville.edu/
http://www.englib.cornell.edu/ice/
http://www.haverford.edu/library/reference/mschaus/mfi/
    mfi.html

http://www.national-academies.org/
http://www.info.lib.uh.edu/wj/webjour.html
http://www.lib.umich.edu/govdocs/stats.html
http://www.ibiblio.org/slanews/internet/archives.html
http://www.ibiblio.org/slanews/internet/archives.html
http://www.yourdictionary.com
http://www.calvin.edu/library/searreso/internet/asl
http://www.hw.ac.uk/libWWW/irn/pinakes/pinakes.
   html
http://www.humbul.ac.uk/
http://www.bubl.ac.uk

Chapter 11 Intelligent agents

http://bots.internet.com/search/s-chat.htm
http://www.alexlit.com/
http://www.tnrdlib.bc.ca/rr.html
http://www.amazon.com
http://www.moviecritic.com/
http//ai.iit.nrc.ca/II_public/WebBird/tryIt.html
http://www.botspot.com/s-search.htm
http://www.copernic.com
http://www.lexibot.com/
http://www.brightplanet.com
http://www.alexa.com
http://www.crayon.net
http://nt.excite.com/
http://www.infogate.com/
http://www.aj.com
http://www.yahoo.com
http://www.hotbot.lycos.co.uk/index.html?coomo.x=1

Chapter 12 Usenet newsgroups and
mailing lists

http://www.faq.org
http://www.faq.org/faqs/usenet/
http://groups.google.com/
http://www.yahoo.com/Computers_and_Internet/
   Software/Internet/Usenet
http://www.forteinc.com

http://www.topica.com
http://paml.net/
http://www.alastra.com/paml/indexes.html
http://www.tile.net/
http://www.meta-list.net/
http://www.ifla.org/l/training/listserv/lists.htm
http://clubs.yahoo.com/
http://www.jiscmail.ac.uk
http://www.jisc.ac.uk

Chapter 13 The information mix and into the future

http://www.dyslexiaonline.com/center.html
http://www.imdb.com
http://www.metaplus.com
http://www.dailywav.com/
http://www.jiscmail.ac.uk
http://www.mailbase.ac.uk
http://www.open.gov.uk
http://www.ukonline.gov.uk
http://www.timeout.co.uk
http://www.odci.gov/cia/publications/factbook/
http://www.usatoday.com
http://www.britannica.com
http://www.bartleby.com/65/
http://www.amazon.com
http://www.dataware.com
http://www.pulver.com/million/
http://www.infogate.com/

Chapter 14 Forty tips and hints for better and quicker searching

http://www.theregister.co.uk/content/6/15501.html
http://news.bbc.co.uk/hi/english/sci/tech/
    newsid_790000/790685.stm
http://mindit.netmind.com/
http://www.philb.com/
http://www.adobe.com/products/acrobat/readstep.html

Chapter 15 Sources for further help and assistance

http://www.catholic-forum.com/saints/pst01058.htm
http://www.searchenginewatch.com
http://webreference.com/
http://events.internet.com
http://www.conferences.calendar.com
http://browserwatch.internet.com
http://www.internetNews.com/
http://www.cnet.com
http://www.zdnet.com/
http://www.december.com/cmc/info/
http://thelist.internet.com/
http://www.thedirectory.org/
http://www.jesus.com
http://HoaxBusters.ciac.org/
http://www.fau.edu/netiquette/netiquette.html
http://www.matisse.net/files/glossary.html
http://www.jiscmail.ac.uk
http://www.topica.com
http://www.junkemail.org/scamspam/
http://www.ftc.gov
http://www.claws-and-paws.com/spam-l/
http://spam.abuse.net/
http://www.dis.strath.ac.uk/business/search.html
http://www.unn.ac.uk/central/isd/features.htm
http://www.notess.com/search/
http://www.monash.com/spidap.html
http://www.mlb.ilstu.edu/ressubj/subject/intrnet/
    srcheng.html
http://www.philb.com
http://news.cnet.com/news/
    0-1003-200-6029873.html?tag=tp_pr
http://www.internetwk.com/
http://biz.yahoo.com/news/Internet.html
http://www.cs.rochester.edu/u/ferguson/
    announce.www/
http://wwwscout.cs.wisc.edu/scout/report
http://www.amazon.com
http://bookshop.blackwell.co.uk
http://www.onlinebooksearch.com

http://www.tucows.com
http://www.qbc. clic.net/~mephisto/bush/ bush.html
http://operasoftware.com
http://www.spycatcher.com
http://www.magnusbrading.com/bmc/
http://www.moonsoftware.ee
http://www.aeria.com/products/index.htm
http://webstripper.com/
http://www.evolve.co.uk/unmozify
http://www.real.com
http://www.adobe.com
http://quicktime.apple.com/
http://abcnews.go.com/sections/tech/DailyNews/
　　virus000530.html
http://www.symantic.co.uk/region/uk/product/
　　navbrochure/
http://www.drsolomon.com
http://www.mcafee.com/
http://www.eliashim.com
http://housecall.antivirus.com/
http://www.zonelabs.com
http://www.ala.org
http://www.aslib.co.uk
http://www.cla.amlibs.ca
http://www.ifla.org
http://www.la-hq.org.uk
http://www.tfpl.com
http://www.yahoo.com/Computers_and_Internet/
　　Internet/News_and_Media/Magazines/

Index